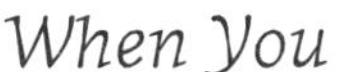

RECIPES FOR CELEBRATIONS

Recipes for Celebrations

Natale Adriano Fasciani

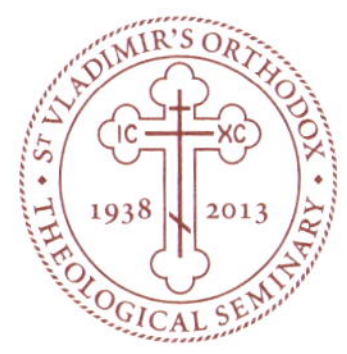

ST VLADIMIR'S SEMINARY PRESS
Crestwood, New York
2013

Library of Congress Control Number: 2013953600

When You Feast: Recipes for Celebrations

St Vladimir's Seminary Press
575 Scarsdale Road
Yonkers, New York
www.svspress.com
800-204-2665

PRINTED IN THE UNITED STATES OF AMERICA

Table of Contents

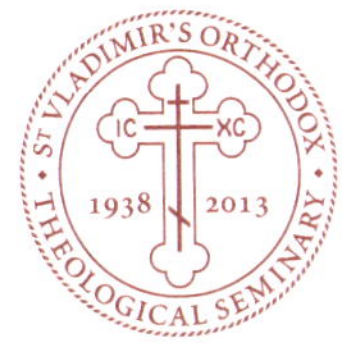

Foreword

"And the Lord appeared to him (Abraham) by the oaks of Mamre, as he sat at the door of his tent in the heat of the day. He lifted up his eyes and looked, and behold, three men stood in front of him. When he saw them, he ran from the tent door to meet them, and bowed himself to the earth, and said, 'My lord, if I have found favor in your sight, do not pass by your servant. Let a little water be brought, and wash your feet, and rest yourselves under the tree, while I fetch a morsel of bread, that you may refresh yourselves, and after that you may pass on—since you have come to your servant.' And Abraham hastened into the tent to Sarah, and said, 'Make ready three measures of fine meal, knead it, and make cakes.' And Abraham ran to the herd and took a calf, tender and good, and gave it to a servant, who hastened to prepare it. Then he took curds, and milk, and the calf which he had prepared, and set it before them; and he stood by them under the tree while they ate" (Gen. 18:1–8).

It is no accident that Abraham's first reflex when he saw the three angels of the Lord while sitting beneath the oaks of Mamre was to jump to his feet and to offer them food. Sharing food is a very human thing to do. It is an act that demonstrates a very ancient understanding of food as more than just the intake of calories. The sharing of food is a sign of "belonging" and an expression of friendship that is something uniquely human.

Since the earliest times, hospitality (*philoxenia*—literally "the love of strangers") has been expressed by the sharing of food. Wherever I have been in the world, be it Alaska or Africa, I have been made welcome, included, by the sharing of food. Even in the most primitive cultures, strangers are made to feel at rest and peace by the simple act of sharing a meal. When someone, friend or stranger, comes into my home, I have this urge to feed him or her. My reflex, like Abraham's, is to feed people when they come to my home. It is one of the ways I show people I love them.

I remember traveling in Alaska to the village a Napaskiak. A walrus, something considered to be a local delicacy, had apparently made a wrong turn and swam up the Kuskokwim River toward the village. One of the local Yup'ik hunters killed it and shared it with the other people of the village. And, as I happened to be there as well, he was very proud to have offered a piece to me as a gesture of welcome. Now, walrus it not something I eat every day. But, I ate some as a sign of my gratitude. This same,–very human and very ancient,–ritual of kindness, generosity and, thanksgiving is repeated every day in almost every culture and place.

Meals are also vehicles by which communities demonstrate their accord and harmony. We celebrate the great events of life using food. The great American feast is Thanksgiving. The busiest days of the year for airports and on our highways are those around Thanksgiving, as families go to great lengths to make sure everyone is together to share a holiday meal. I remember the great kindness of my fellow seminary students when they invited me to their homes to eat with their families on this one day when America as a nation gives thanks for all the blessings God has showered upon us. And we renew and deepen our ties with our family and friends by feasting together.

We also pass on our family traditions at these holidays. One could really say that more than just the body is nourished at holiday tables. We bring out our cherished family recipes and in doing so we reach back through time to the tables our parents and grandparents set in years

past. Christmastime is about the only time I make cakes of Scottish shortbread to give to those I love as gifts. And, as I make each one, I remember my Granny. This simple act of combining flour, butter and sugar somehow makes someone who is long gone present and brings us together by means of an act of love and sharing that has been passed down from one generation to another in my family.

With this in mind, it is not difficult to understand that it is also a table that stands at the very heart of our Orthodox Christian Faith. I love to tell children there is a table in the altar. It is a very special table, God's table, but it is a table all the same. And on this table are the very same things we have on our tables at home: a placemat, a plate, a cup, a knife, a spoon, and a napkin. And we, the people of God, His family, gather around this table to share a common meal, the Marriage Supper of the Lamb.

God gives us grapes and wheat. We take them and do something only humans can do. We make them into wine and bread. We then offer them back to God and He once again returns them to us as His Body and Blood. He offers Himself to us as life-sustaining food. To take part in this meal is a sign of community, of belonging, and an expression of mutual peace. We are God's family gathered around His table. The very word "communion" expresses so well the mystery of our being together with God and the saints of every time and place in His Kingdom at His Great Supper as one family. And Christ, the only High Priest, stands at the head of this table and presides at this meal. He is the One who is offered and the One who offers.

We Americans live in a culture that is quickly losing its connection with food. Very few of us know where our food comes from. And very few of us "dine." Most of us inhale our food. We even have this odd term: "fast food." It is food eaten on the run, in a car or in front of the television, mindlessly and almost without tasting it. It is the norm today. The table, as a place where families gather and share their lives and life, is fast becoming a rarity. It is no wonder we have begun to become isolated, lonely, and disconnected from one another. We have lost the simple, ancient concept of food as sacrament, as something holy, given to us by God that can bring us together.

Some of my fondest memories of my time as a student at St. Vladimir's are connected to the seminary kitchen. I recall my first Pascha as a student. Everyone was assigned some duty to prepare the community for the Paschal night. I was assigned to the kitchen. I worked together with about eight others assisting Tina, the cook, roasting meats, slicing them, and doing the hundred little things that would result in a wonderful banquet for the entire seminary community, staff, and students. We did not eat horseradish in my family. I had no idea that it came in any other form than a jar. Tina asked if someone would grate the horseradish. I, innocently, volunteered. I was handed three rather odd looking roots that had been peeled and shown the commercial mixer onto which had been placed the meat grinding attachment. Then everyone slipped out of the small room leaving me alone with the strange vegetable and the grinder. I put the first piece into the machine and in seconds it was as though some sort of poison gas had been released into the kitchen. My eyes were watering, my nose running, and my lungs burning! And people were going to eat that stuff! And now, whenever I eat horseradish, I am instantly transported to that little room and the grinder.

It was these sorts of experiences that formed in me a love of the community, a community gathered together around a table. And I began to understand the power of the table to foster a sense of belonging. As a bishop, I was faced with a problem in a small, struggling mission far away from the rest of the diocese, in Kona, HI. The priest had to leave, and I realized it was going to be at least a year until I could get another priest to take care of the mission. What would we do? How could we keep this small group together? I told them to do three things: meet every Sunday at the same time and place without fail, read the Scripture readings appointed for that day and discuss them, and eat together. And, by God's grace, they were able to stay together until such time as a new pastor could be assigned.

Mr. Fasciani's book expresses a love for food. Nat has learned to negotiate the sometimes complicated labyrinth of Orthodox Christian dietary rules while graciously allowing for the tastes, likes, and dislikes of those for whom he cooks. If an army travels on its stomach, it can certainly be said that a school studies on it. And so, Mr. Fasciani shares his love of food and the community he serves through the recipes presented in this book.

I hope the recipes in this book will enrich your own table and community.

+Benjamin

Archbishop of San Francisco

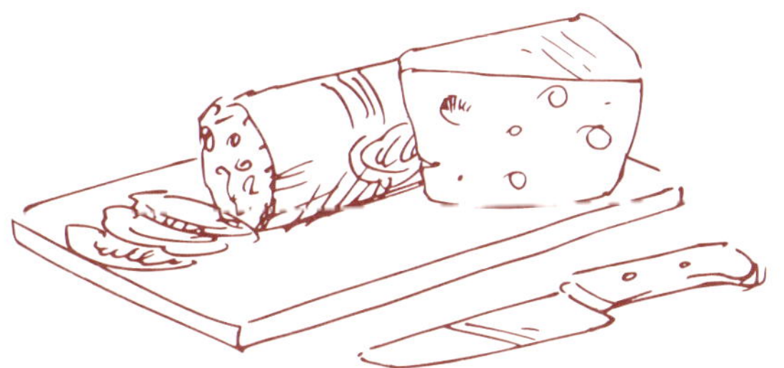

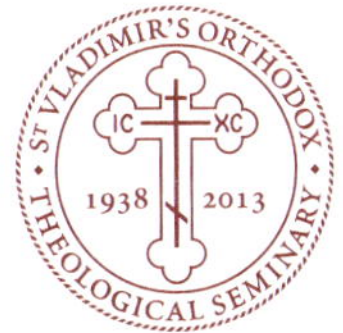

Breads

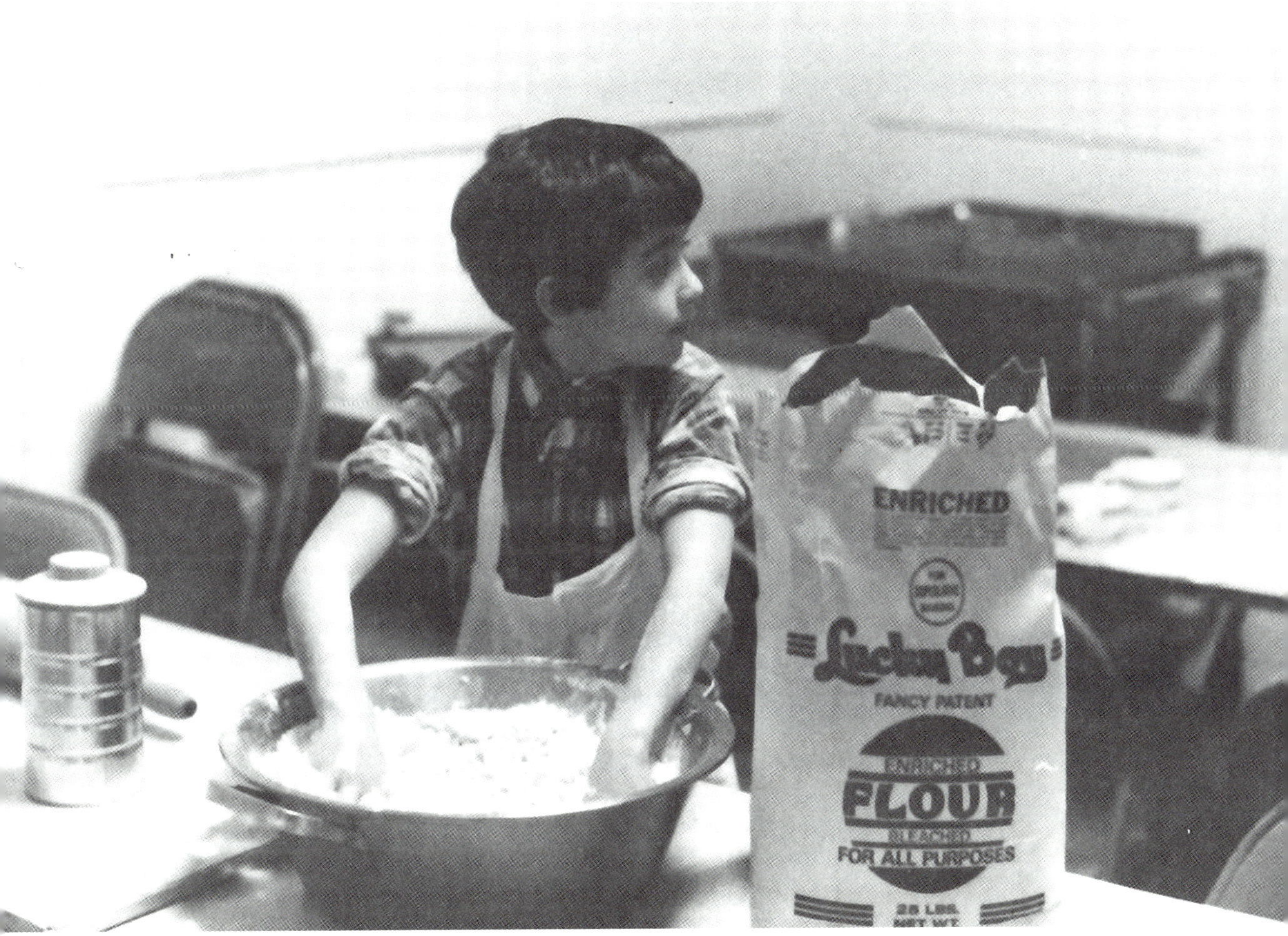
ENRICHED
Lucky Boy
FANCY PATENT
ENRICHED
FLOUR
BLEACHED
FOR ALL PURPOSES

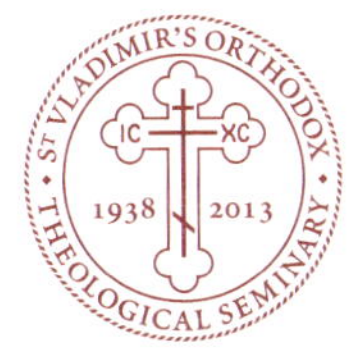

Ciabatta Bread

- **1½ teaspoons active dry yeast**
- **5 tablespoons warm milk**
- **1 cup plus 3 tablespoons water, room temperature**
- **2 tablespoons olive oil**
- **4 cups unbleached flour**
- **1 tablespoon cornmeal**
- **½ teaspoon salt**

Stir yeast into the milk and let it sit for 10–13 minutes.

In a mixer with paddle, mix water, olive oil, and half of the flour.

Knead for 2–3 minutes on low speed, slowly adding more flour.

Increase speed to medium, and at this point the dough will look and feel stickier and softer than normal bread dough.

Add the salt and the rest of the flour.

Switch to dough hook; knead for 5–6 minutes more.

Place the dough in a lightly greased bowl; cover it with plastic wrap, and set it in a warm place for about 1 hour, more or less, until it doubles in size.

Place the dough on a well–floured surface and cut it into 4 equal pieces.

Roll each piece into a log shape and stretch it out, pressing it into a rectangle shape about 9×5 inches. The dough may feel too sticky; it works better if you coat your hands with a little oil. Repeat the same with the other 3 pieces.

Dust well with flour. Prepare 4 pieces of parchment paper and place dough on the parchment. Cover with a damp cloth and let it rise again, until not quite doubled.

Preheat oven to 425F.

Invert the dough onto a well-greased baking sheet pan and bake for 20–25 minutes, or until golden brown. For a nice crust, spray ciabatta 3–4 times with a water mister during the first 12 minutes of baking.

Let it rest at room temperature for 10 minutes before cutting.

Coconut Corn Bread

2 cups coarse cornmeal
1 tablespoon baking powder
½ teaspoon salt
1¼ cups coconut milk
¼ cup shredded coconut
2 eggs
¼ cup melted butter

Preheat oven to 400F.

In a bowl, mix together the cornmeal, baking powder, and salt. In a separate bowl, whisk the coconut milk and eggs, and add them to the dry mixture. Add the butter and shredded coconut; pour into a greased baking pan about 8×8 inches, and bake for 25–30 minutes, or until light brown and firm.

Cool, and slice to serve.

Corn Bread with Jalapeño

3 cups corn bread mix
2½ cups milk
1 small can cream of corn
6-ounce can of jalapeños
1½ cups cheddar cheese, grated
1 onion grated
½ cup olive oil
3 eggs beaten
1 teaspoon sugar

Preheat oven to 450F.

In a bowl, mix milk, oil, eggs, sugar, onion, corn, jalapeños, and cheese, add to the corn bread mix and mix well. Pour into 2 round, greased pans.

Bake 25–30 minutes, or until a toothpick comes out clean. Let the bread cool, then slice and serve.

Basic Pizza Dough

2 teaspoons active dry yeast
1 teaspoon sugar
1¼ cups warm water (110F)
3⅓ cups unbleached all-purpose flour
1½ teaspoons salt
3 teaspoons extra virgin olive oil

In a small bowl, dissolve the yeast and the sugar, and allow it to "work" for 6–7 minutes (you will see bubbles).

Place the dough blade in a food processor; add flour, salt, 2 teaspoons olive oil.

With machine running, pour liquid through top hole as fast as flour absorbs it.

Process until dough rolls clean off the bowl, then process additional 30–40 seconds to knead the dough.

At this point the dough may be a little sticky; coat the dough with 1 teaspoon oil.

Transfer into an oiled plastic container, cover with plastic wrap, and let it rise for 45–50 minutes at warm room temperature.

It's ready to use with your favorite pizza recipe!

Pizza Bread Rosemary

One 1-pound pizza dough
2 tablespoons extra virgin olive oil
½ teaspoon rosemary
1 clove garlic, peeled and crushed
Kosher salt and pepper to taste

Preheat oven to 375F.

On a lightly floured surface, stretch the dough to about 12–14 inches in diameter.

With a fork, prick the top of the dough several times, so it won't bubble up during the cooking process.

In a food processor, blend well the oil, rosemary, garlic, salt, and pepper.

Place the stretched dough on a lightly floured baking sheet pan.

Brush the blended mixture over the top.

Bake for 12–17 minutes, or until fully cooked.

Serve hot or at room temperature.

Walnut Banana Bread

3 cups all-purpose flour
2 cups sugar
1 teaspoon baking powder
1 teaspoon salt
¾ teaspoon allspice
½ teaspoon baking soda
½ teaspoon ground cinnamon
4 eggs
1 cup vegetable oil
3 teaspoons vanilla extract
1½ cups grated yellow and green zucchini (mix)
1 cup grated carrots
2 cups mashed ripe bananas
1 cup golden raisins
1 cup chopped walnuts

Preheat oven to 350F.

In a mixing bowl, mix together flour, sugar, baking powder, salt, allspice, baking soda, and ground cinnamon. Add eggs, oil, and vanilla, then mix well. Add zucchini, carrots, banana, and mix for a minute; add raisins and walnuts.

Pour the mixture into four well-greased and floured loaf pans. Bake for 45–50 minutes, or until a toothpick comes out clean, then cool for 15 minutes and remove from pans.

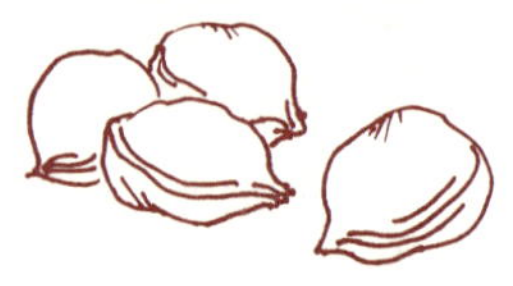

Zucchini and Banana Bread

4 ripe bananas, peeled
1½ cups grated zucchini (green)
1½ cups grated carrots
1 cup golden raisins
1 cup chopped walnuts
1 cup vegetable oil
4 eggs
3 cups flour
2 cups sugar
1 teaspoon baking powder
1 teaspoon allspice
½ teaspoon baking soda
½ teaspoon ground cinnamon
1 teaspoon salt
3 teaspoons vanilla extract

Preheat oven to 350F.

In a mixing bowl, mix together flour, sugar, baking powder, allspice, baking soda, and cinnamon. Alternately add the eggs, vanilla, oil, walnuts, raisins, carrots, and zucchini, then add bananas, one at a time, and keep mixing for 2–3 minutes until well mixed.

Place the mixture in a well greased 9×13 pan and bake for 55–60 minutes. If the bread starts to brown too much, cover it with aluminum foil and cook until a toothpick comes out clean and dry. Let it cool for 15 minutes, cut into squares and serve.

Makes 16–20 portions.

Zucchini-Walnut Raisin Bread

3 whole eggs
2 cups sugar
1 cup vegetable oil
2 cups grated yellow and green zucchini with skin on, seeded
3 teaspoons vanilla
3 cups flour
½ teaspoon baking powder
1 teaspoon salt
1 teaspoon baking soda
3 teaspoons ground cinnamon
1 cup chopped walnuts
1 cup raisin

Preheat oven to 350F.

In a bowl, beat eggs, then add sugar, vegetable oil, zucchini, and vanilla.

Mix together the flour, baking powder, salt, baking soda, and cinnamon, and add to the zucchini mixture.

When well combined, add the chopped nuts and raisins, and pour into 2 9×5 loaf pans, well-greased.

Bake for 1 hour or until done.

Appetizers

ST VLADIMIR'S ORTHODOX
THEOLOGICAL SEMINARY
IC XC
1938 2013

Bacon-Wrapped Scallops

10 medium sized scallops
10 long strips of bacon
2 tablespoons olive oil
2 tablespoons melted butter
pinch of garlic powder, cayenne, and black pepper
10 wooden toothpicks
1 tablespoon chopped parsley

Preheat oven to 400F.

Mix olive oil, butter, garlic powder, cayenne and black pepper, and blend well.

Toss scallops into the mixture .

Wrap bacon around scallops and secure with toothpicks.

Place in a baking pan and bake for 20–25 minutes or until bacon is well done.

Serve with sweet and sour sauce, and wedges of lemon.

Garnish with chopped parsley.

Bruschetta Black Olive Spread

10 slices baguette bread cut into ¼-inch thick rounds
4 tablespoons extra virgin olive oil, plus 2 more
¼ cup pitted black olives
3–4 anchovies
3–4 sun-dried tomatoes soaked for 10 minutes and drained
2–3 leaves of fresh basil
1 clove garlic peeled
1½ tablespoons sour cream
black pepper

Lightly grease bread rounds on both sides with some of the oil.

Toast or grill them on both sides, and then place them on a platter to cool.

Place all the remaining olive oil, olives, anchovies, sun-dried tomatoes, fresh basil, garlic, sour cream, and black pepper in a food processor, blend well for 15–20 seconds until the mixture acquires the consistency of a spread.

Divide the spread among the 10 slices of bread and serve.

Bruschetta with Tomatoes

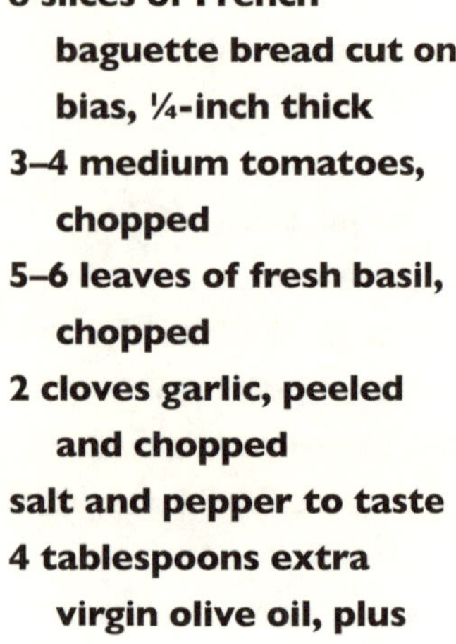

8 slices of French baguette bread cut on bias, ¼-inch thick
3–4 medium tomatoes, chopped
5–6 leaves of fresh basil, chopped
2 cloves garlic, peeled and chopped
salt and pepper to taste
4 tablespoons extra virgin olive oil, plus 3 more for brushing

Brush both sides of bread with olive oil.

Bake or grill bread on both sides until slightly toasted.

Lay them on a serving platter.

Mix together tomatoes, basil, garlic, salt, pepper, and remaining oil.

Spoon onto the bread and serve.

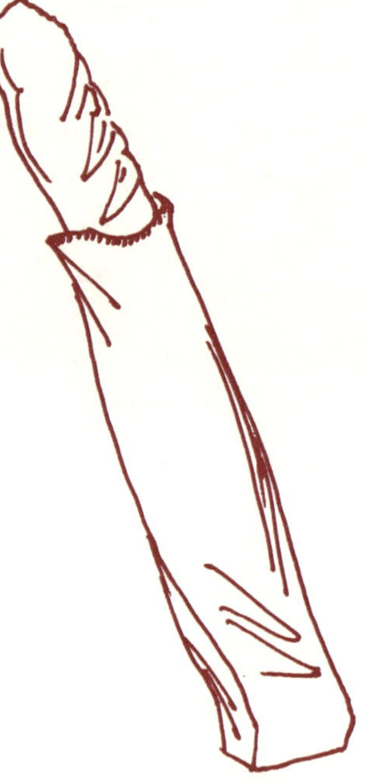

Caprese (Tomatoes and Mozzarella)

On a round serving dish, arrange tomatoes, mozzarella, and basil in an alternating pattern.

Drizzle with oil, and season with salt and pepper.

TIP: If buffalo mozzarella is not available, regular mozzarella will do just fine.

10 slices of beefsteak tomatoes ¼-inch thick
10 slices buffalo mozzarella ¼-inch thick
10 leaves fresh basil
5–6 tablespoons extra virgin olive oil
salt and pepper to taste

Chocolate Chip Nachos

10 (6-inch) flour tortillas
½ teaspoon cinnamon
¼ cup granulated sugar
½ cup butter, melted
¾ cup chocolate chips

Preheat oven to 350F.

Mix together sugar and cinnamon, and place in a shallow dish; set aside.

Brush the tortillas with melted butter on both sides, then dip them into the sugar mixture, coating them well. Cut the tortillas into 6 wedges. Spread these out in a baking pan and bake for 10 minutes or until light brown.

In the meantime, melt chocolate over low heat or in a microwave.

Spread the wedges on a serving dish, drizzle with melted chocolate, and serve.

TIP: Form a "sandwich" by placing chocolate between two nachos; or top each nacho with half a strawberry, or two raspberries, and so on—be creative! Great snack!

Eggs Stuffed with Crabmeat

Keep half of the parsley aside for garnish.

Peel the eggs, cut lengthwise, and remove the yolks; set the whites aside for the moment. Mash the yolks with the remaining ingredients to form a paste-like substance.

Stuff each egg half with the filling—use a piping-bag for better presentation.

Cover and refrigerate until ready to serve, then sprinkle with remaining parsley.

6 hard-boiled eggs
¾ cup crabmeat
½ stalk celery finely chopped
1 tablespoon mayonnaise
¼ teaspoon minced garlic
¾ teaspoon fresh parsley
salt and pepper to taste
1 teaspoon dry mustard
Tabasco sauce to taste

Gibanica (Serbian Style)

1 pound phyllo dough (room temperature)
2 pounds feta cheese (crumbled in small pieces)
1 cup sour cream
6 large eggs
½ pound melted butter
½ cup all-purpose flour
1 teaspoon salt

Preheat oven to 325F.

In a mixing bowl, beat the eggs, then add flour and sour cream and mix well.

Fold in the feta cheese. Grease a 9×13 pan and place 2 sheets of phyllo dough in the pan. Brush 2 tablespoons of butter onto the dough and spread 6 tablespoons of the cheese mixture on top, repeating layers until all the mixture is used. Top with 2 sheets of phyllo, brushing with remaining butter.

Bake for about 1 hour; when the crust starts to brown and the cheese doesn't jiggle when you shake the pan, then it should be done. If not, cover with aluminum foil and cook some more.

Let it cool at room temperature, cut it in squares or in a diamond shape, and serve.

Grilled Fresh Figs

10 fresh figs (large if possible), cut in half lengthwise
10 shelled walnuts
8 ounces goat cheese
3–4 tablespoons balsamic vinegar

Get grill nice and hot, lightly greased.

Place figs on grill open face down, for about 10–15 seconds (do not burn!).

Place them on a rack or paper towel to cool to room temperature.

Divide goat cheese onto the 10 figs (grilled side).

Top with walnut, drizzle with balsamic vinegar, and serve.

Make Your Own Nachos

10 flour tortillas
2 cups vegetable oil for frying
Kosher salt for seasoning

Preheat oil to 400F. Cut tortillas into 6 wedges, then divide chips into several batches.

Fry each batch about 1 minute or until light golden brown, stirring constantly. Repeat for each batch, placing each on a paper towel to drain. Season with salt and serve with your favorite dip.

Middle Eastern Pizza

4 pieces pita bread (no packet)
1 cup marinara sauce or tomato sauce
1½ cups mixed shredded mozzarella, cheddar, and Swiss chees

Preheat oven to 375F.

Place pita bread on a sheet pan, spread the sauce on top, and add the cheese mixture.

Bake for about 15 minutes, or until hot and the cheese is melted. Cut in half, and serve.

TIP: Add other toppings and be creative!

Stuffed Avocado

- **2 ripe avocados**
- **juice of 2 limes**
- **4 tablespoons plain yogurt**
- **1 tomato, seeded and chopped**
- **1 teaspoon chopped cilantro**
- **½ jalapeño pepper, seeded and chopped**
- **salt and pepper to taste**

Split avocado in half and discard the pit. With a spoon, scoop out the pulp and chop it, saving the shell. Mix together lime juice, yogurt, tomato, cilantro, and jalapeño and season with salt and pepper. Spoon the mixture evenly back into the 4 avocado shells, and serve.

Garnish with a sprig of fresh cilantro.

TIP: Serve this with nacho chips on the side.

Serves 4.

Breakfast

ST VLADIMIR'S ORTHODOX
THEOLOGICAL SEMINARY
IC XC
1938 2013

Sun-Dried Tomatoes and Eggs

8 sun-dried tomatoes soaked in water for 10 minutes, then drained and chopped
4 tablespoons olive oil
1 small onion, chopped
6 eggs
½ cup grated parmesan cheese
1 tablespoon chopped parsley
salt and pepper to taste
4 tablespoons milk

In a non-stick skillet, heat oil.

Sauté onion 2–3 minutes, until soft.

Add the chopped sun-dried tomatoes.

Sauté 2–3 minutes more.

Beat the eggs, add milk, and pour into the pan.

Add the cheese, mix it well, cook on medium heat about 5–6 minutes.

When the mixture starts to brown, use a large spatula and flip the frittata to the other side.

Cook for 3–4 minutes more, or until fully cooked.

TIP: Go easy on the salt (because of the cheese) and use a pinch of black pepper.

Baked Frittata (omelet)

16 jumbo eggs, scrambled
2 cups milk
1 cup cooked ham, chopped in small pieces
1 cup shredded cheddar cheese
1 cup shredded mozzarella
2 tablespoons minced onion
1 cup sliced mushrooms
2 cloves garlic
3 tablespoons olive oil
1 teaspoon butter
1 tablespoon fresh chopped parsley
salt and pepper to taste

Preheat oven to 350F.

Scramble the eggs in a mixing bowl, then add milk and chopped parsley. Season with salt and pepper. Add the ham and cheese.

In a frying pan, heat the oil and butter and sauté the onions, garlic, and mushrooms until soft.

Add to the egg mixture and toss all ingredients; pour into an 8×10 greased baking pan and bake uncovered for 35–40 minutes, or until the eggs are cooked and firm.

Floating Eggs

4 large eggs
4 slices whole wheat bread
2–3 tablespoons butter
1 tablespoon chopped chives
salt and pepper to taste

Cut a round hole in the center of the bread, about 2½ inches in diameter.

Brush butter on both sides of the bread and place bread on a hot skillet for about 2–3 minutes, or until light brown.

Flip bread to other side and start browning the other side.

In the meantime, break an egg into each hole and cook the eggs 2–3 minutes until done; place the bread with the eggs in serving dishes and top with chopped chives.

TIP: These are delicious when served with home fries.

Serves 4.

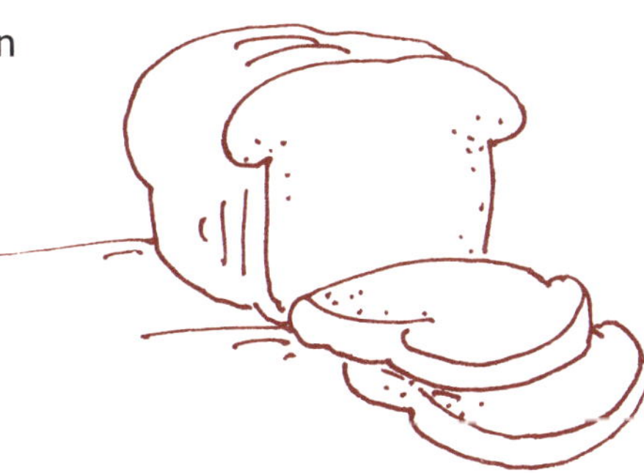

Quiche

1 9-inch unbaked pie crust
¾ cup shredded cheddar cheese
¾ cup shredded Swiss cheese
1 teaspoon flour
¾ cup diced cooked ham, chopped cooked bacon, or combination of both
3 eggs, beaten
1 cup milk
1 tablespoon chopped fresh parsley
1 tablespoon chopped pimento (optional)
salt and pepper to taste

Preheat oven to 400F.

Mix together the cheeses, flour, and parsley. In a separate bowl, mix egg and milk, season with salt and pepper, and set aside

With a pastry brush, brush the pie crust with some of the egg mix. Place half the cheese in bottom of pie crust, add the meat, and add pimento (optional). Top with remainder of the cheese and pour the egg mixture over the cheese, making sure the mixture is lower than the rim. Place quiche on a sheet pan for easy handling, and bake for 50–55 minutes, or until it sets and the crust is golden brown.

Serves 6.

Fried Halloumi Cheese

½ cup extra virgin oil
1 pound of halloumi cheese, cut into 1 inch thick slices
Arab flatbread
2 pounds tomatoes, sliced

In a skillet, bring oil to medium hot.

Place slices of cheese in oil until browned on one side, then turn to other side and brown as well.

Drain and serve hot, with Arab flatbread and sliced tomatoes.

Soup

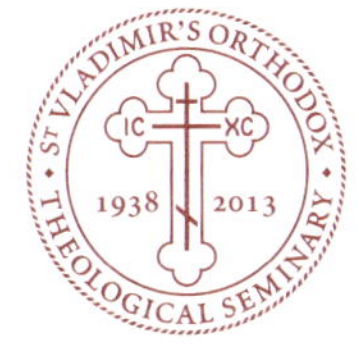

ST VLADIMIR'S ORTHODOX THEOLOGICAL SEMINARY
IC XC
1938 2013

Butternut Squash Soup

3 tablespoons extra virgin olive oil
½ stick butter
1 large onion, peeled and chopped
1 large fennel bulb, cleaned and chopped
2 stalks celery, washed and chopped
1 large butternut squash, peeled, seeded, and chopped
2 large carrots, peeled and chopped
7–8 cups chicken broth
salt and white pepper to taste

Heat oil and butter in a large pot, then add onions, fennel, celery, squash, and carrots. Sauté for 10 minutes or so, stirring occasionally; add chicken broth to cover the vegetables, then cover the pot, and cook until all vegetables are very tender and mushy. Once all is cooked, add the salt and pepper to taste, and process the soup in a food processor to make an even, smooth, thick soup. If you prefer a thinner soup, you can blend in more broth.

Garnish with a few fresh mint leaves.

Cold Melon Soup

In a food processor, purée the melon, lime juice, and orange juice; stir in club soda, checking for consistency.

Chill well and serve.

Add some sugar only if needed, according to taste.

Garnish with mint leaf.

3 cups ripe cantaloupe
3 cups honeydew melon
1 cup fresh orange juice
⅓ cup fresh lime juice
2 cups club soda (less for a thicker soup)
sugar to taste
fresh mint leaves

Cream of Avocado Soup

2 ripe avocados
juice of 1 lemon
1½ cups buttermilk
1½ cups low-fat milk
1 red bell pepper, seeded and finely chopped
2 scallions, green only, thinly sliced
2 tablespoons fresh chopped dill
2 tablespoons fresh chopped parsley
½ teaspoon ground cumin
½ teaspoon curry powder
sea salt and pepper to taste

Mash well the avocados with lemon juice, stir in the buttermilk and enough low-fat milk to achieve a slightly thick consistency. Stir in the remaining seasonings and herbs, mix well, cover and chill in refrigerator.

Garnish with fresh sprig of dill.

Serve cold.

Serves 4.

French Onion Soup

3 tablespoons extra virgin olive oil
8–9 medium size onions peeled, cut in half, and thinly sliced
3 cloves garlic, peeled and minced
½ cup dry white wine
1 teaspoon dry mustard
4 tablespoons miso paste, dissolved in ¼ cup warm water
6 slices French bread cut on the bias, 1-inch thick, then toasted or baked, hard and crisp
¾ pounds shredded mozzarella
5–6 cups water

Preheat oven to 350F.

Heat oil in a large soup pot, add onions, and sauté over low heat until golden brown. Add garlic and sauté for an additional minute; add water, wine, and mustard. Bring to a boil, then simmer for 15 minutes, stirring in the dissolved miso. Remove from heat; allow to stand for 10–15 minutes.

Arrange one piece of the bread in each ovenproof soup bowl. Ladle a serving of the soup over each one. Sprinkle the mozzarella cheese over the top of each bowl; place the bowls on a sheet pan for easy handling. Bake the soup for 10–12 minutes or until the cheese is fully melted and starts to brown. Serve hot.

Serves 6.

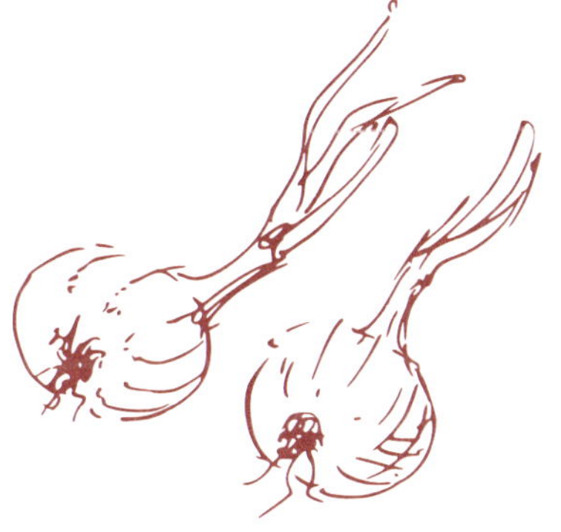

Fruit Soup

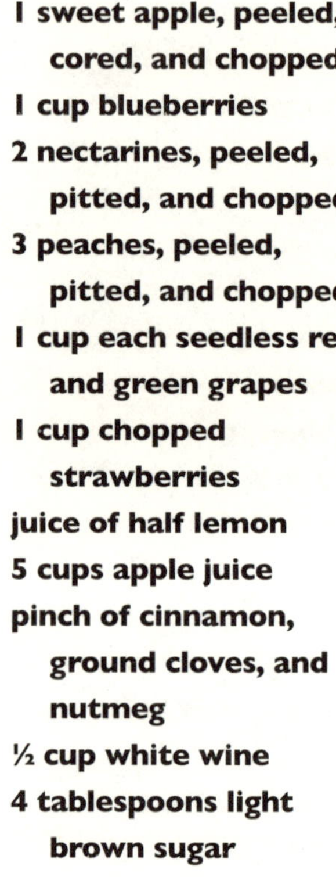

1 sweet apple, peeled, cored, and chopped
1 cup blueberries
2 nectarines, peeled, pitted, and chopped
3 peaches, peeled, pitted, and chopped
1 cup each seedless red and green grapes
1 cup chopped strawberries
juice of half lemon
5 cups apple juice
pinch of cinnamon, ground cloves, and nutmeg
½ cup white wine
4 tablespoons light brown sugar
sprigs of fresh mint

In a large pot, combine all ingredients but fresh mint, and bring to a boil. Simmer over low heat, covered, for 20–25 minutes, until the fruit is tender. Allow to cool for 10–15 minutes. Pulse a few times in a food processor, and chill in refrigerator.

Stir before serving and garnish with fresh mint.

TIP: If needed, add more brown sugar for sweetness, or more apple juice for consistency.

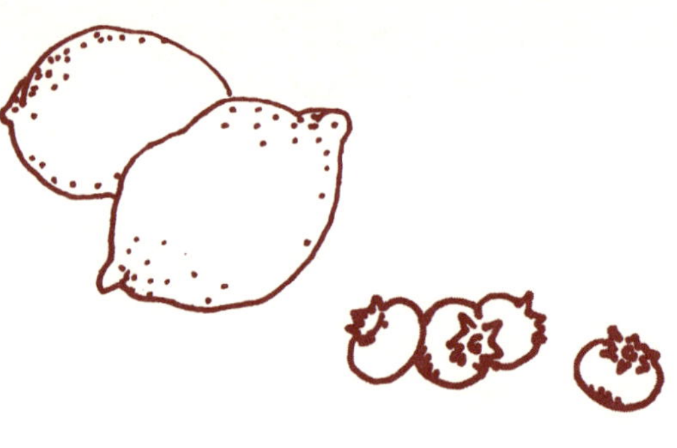

Gazpacho

Mix all the ingredients in large bowl, then pulse in a food processor only several times, until consistent—yet still with a little crunchy bite! If necessary, do this in several batches.

Chill at least 2 hours and serve.

Serves 6.

1 14-ounce can plum tomatoes, with liquid
1 cucumber, seeded and chopped
1 green and 1 red bell pepper, seeded and chopped
2 scallions, rinsed and chopped
½ cup chopped parsley
¼ cup chopped fresh dill
3 cups tomato juice
1 large carrot, peeled and chopped
1 stalk celery, cleaned and chopped
juice of 2 lemons
1 tablespoon chili powder
Kosher salt and pepper to taste
dash Tabasco sauce to taste

Jerusalem Artichoke Soup

2 pounds Jerusalem artichokes, scrubbed and diced
3 white potatoes, peeled and diced
1 large onion, peeled and chopped
½ cup white wine
½ teaspoon curry
a pinch of garam masala (optional)
6–7 cups vegetable stock (or hot water with 1 tablespoon chicken base)
2 large leeks, rinsed and chopped (discard the tough green parts)
2 tablespoons butter
¼ cup chopped fresh parsley
juice of 1 lemon
salt and pepper to taste

Place potatoes, onions, wine, curry, leeks, and butter in a large soup pot. Add lemon juice and enough liquid to cover the vegetables. Cover the pot and bring to a boil, then lower heat to simmer. Stir a few times until vegetables are tender, about 20–25 minutes.

In a blender, purée the soup, adding more liquid if it's too thick to create the right consistency. Return to low heat, taste for seasoning, and serve.

Serves 6.

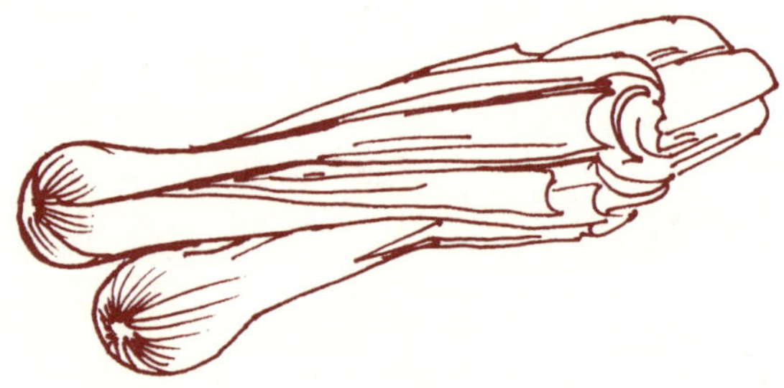

Southern Style Chili Con Carne

- **2½ pounds lean ground beef**
- **⅓ cup olive oil**
- **1 large onion, peeled and chopped**
- **2 jalapeño peppers, seeded and chopped**
- **4 cloves garlic, peeled and chopped**
- **3 14-ounce cans chopped tomatoes with liquid**
- **salt and pepper to taste**
- **½ teaspoon ground cloves**
- **½ teaspoon ground cinnamon**
- **1 tablespoon dry oregano**
- **1 tablespoon paprika**
- **2 tablespoons chili powder**
- **1 tablespoon ground cumin**
- **A few dashes Tabasco sauce**
- **2 15-ounce cans red kidney beans, rinsed and drained**

In a large enough pot, brown the meat, strain the fat and discard, then set the meat aside.

In the same pot heat oil, then sauté onion, garlic, and jalapeño pepper for 3–4 minutes. Add tomatoes and cook for about 10–15 minutes more, then add the rest of seasoning and mix, add the meat back into the sauce, and stir. Check for spiciness, adjust as necessary, then cook for an additional 15–20 minutes. Add beans, continue to cook 15 minutes more, and serve.

TIP: Works well with Mexican rice.

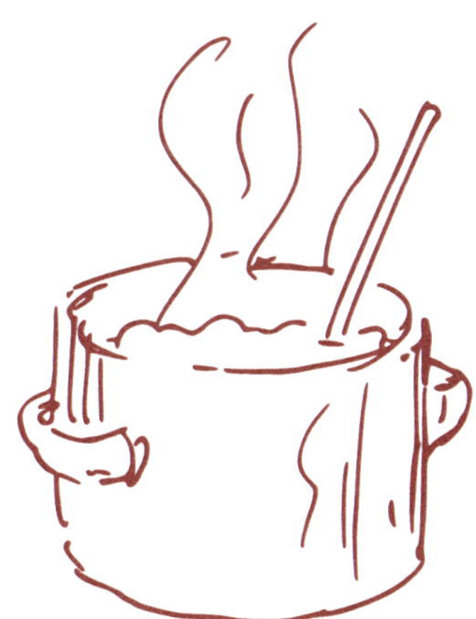

Pasta & Rice

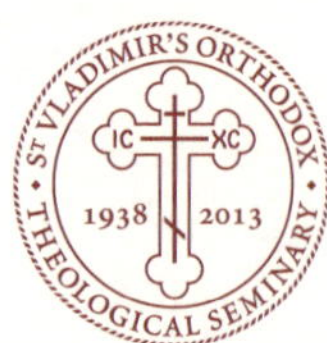

ST VLADIMIR'S ORTHODOX
IC XC
1938 2013
THEOLOGICAL SEMINARY

Amish Chicken Casserole

8–10 ounces egg noodles
2 tablespoons extra virgin olive oil
¼ cup butter
⅓ cup flour
2 cups chicken broth
1 cup milk
⅓ cup grated parmesan cheese
2 cups cooked chicken cut in small pieces, or roughly shredded
salt and pepper to taste
1 tablespoon fresh parsley
pinch of sage

Preheat oven to 350F.

Cook pasta in salted boiling water about 8 minutes, until it is just al dente. Heat oil and butter in a skillet, then sauté the mushrooms for 3 minutes. Stir in the flour; add the milk and chicken broth and mix well with a whisk. Add seasoning and continue to whisk until thickened. Toss noodles in sauce; add chicken pieces and half of the grated cheese; toss.

Place in casserole dish, top with remainder of grated cheese, and bake for 25–30 minutes or until lightly browned.

Garnish with fresh parsley, and serve.

Basic Polenta

6 cups water
1 teaspoon salt
2 cups cornmeal
2–3 tablespoons butter
grated parmesan cheese, to taste
your favorite sauce or toppings

Bring water and salt to a boil and gradually stir in the cornmeal.

Lower the temperature to prevent sticking, and keep stirring occasionally, about 30–35 minutes, or until the mixture becomes thick and the cornmeal is cooked.

Add butter, slowly add the cheese, stir well.

Pour the polenta on a serving platter or in individual serving dishes, top with sauce or garnish, and serve.

TIP: This works for a main dish or as a side dish.

Basmati Rice

1 cup basmati rice, well rinsed
2 cups water
1 teaspoon salt
1 tablespoon butter
2 tablespoons slivered almonds
½ teaspoon ground turmeric
dash ground cumin

Bring water and salt to a boil, add rice, and cook for 5 minutes; add turmeric, cumin, and almonds, and cook for 7–8 minutes more. Check to see if more water is needed; add butter, stir well, and serve.

Serves 4.

Feta Shrimp Pesto Pasta

Cook pasta in salted boiling water. While the pasta is cooking, mix oil, garlic, basil, and pine nuts in a food processor. In a skillet, heat 2 tablespoons of oil and add shrimp, cook for 5–6 minutes. Stir often until shrimp is cooked. Add basil mixture and toss. Drain pasta and add to the sauce and toss; add feta cheese and sliced olives, toss again, and serve.

Garnish with fresh basil leaf.

Serves 4.

1 pound penne rigate
¼ cup extra virgin olive oil, plus 2 tablespoons
4 cloves garlic
¼ cup fresh basil
¼ cup pine nuts, lightly toasted
2 dozen jumbo shrimp, cleaned and deveined
½ cup crumbled feta cheese
salt and pepper to taste
2 tablespoons sliced, pitted Gaeta olives

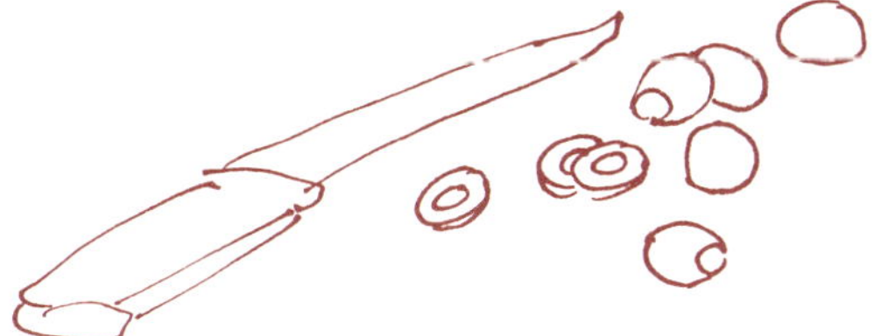

Fettuccine Al Prosciutto (Cured Ham)

1 12-ounce package fettuccine al uovo (made with eggs)
½ cup sliced and chopped prosciutto
¼ cup butter
2 shallots, finely chopped
¾ cup heavy cream
½ cup grated parmesan cheese
black pepper to taste

In a frying pan, heat butter and add the shallots, and cook until soft and lightly browned. Add the prosciutto, stir for 1 minute, season with black pepper, and add heavy cream; simmer first, then keep warm.

Cook the pasta in salted boiling water for about 7–8 minutes (al dente). Drain pasta, add to the sauce, and toss. Add parmesan cheese, and serve hot.

Garnish with fresh sprigs of parsley and black pepper.

Fried Rice Balls (Arancini)

4 cups cooked risotto (any leftover risotto will work just fine)
4 eggs
½ cup shredded mozzarella
¾ cup plain bread crumbs
½ cup flour
oil for deep frying

Beat 2 of the eggs and mix with the rice and some of the bread crumbs.

Start making golf-sized rice balls: take a pinch of mozzarella cheese and press in center of a rice ball, then with the palm of the hand keep rolling it to form a round ball. If too soft, add a little more of the bread crumbs. Once all the rice balls are done, set them aside.

In a bowl, beat the other 2 eggs. Place the bread crumbs on a shallow plate, and the flour on a separate shallow plate. Roll each rice ball first into the flour and then the eggs, then coat each one with bread crumbs. Heat the oil to about 360-370F and start frying the rice balls a few at a time until golden brown and crispy. Drain on paper towels and serve hot.

Fusilli Pasta with Peppers and Onions

1 pound fusilli, penne, or rigatoni
2 red and 2 yellow bell peppers, oven roasted or grilled on all sides, then peeled, seeded, and cut in thin strips
1 large red onion, peeled and thinly sliced
2 cloves garlic, peeled and minced
7 tablespoons extra virgin olive oil
salt and pepper to taste
3 tablespoons fresh chopped parsley
freshly grated parmesan cheese to taste

Cook pasta in boiling, salted water for 8 minutes (until al dente); strain and set aside.

In a large frying pan, heat oil and sauté onion, peppers, and garlic; add a few tablespoons of pasta water.

Add the mixture to the pasta and toss, then add parsley and grated cheese, and serve.

Serves 4.

Linguine Alle Vongole

½ cup extra virgin olive oil
2 large cloves garlic, peeled, mashed, and minced
2½ pounds Manila clams, scrubbed clean
¼ cup dry white wine
½ teaspoon dried hot red pepper (or more to taste)
1 pound thin linguine
¼ cup chopped fresh parsley
¼ cup clam juice
pinch of salt and pepper to taste

In large skillet, heat oil, add clams and toss for 2–3 minutes. Add garlic and toss 1 minute more. Add the wine, clam juice, and hot pepper; reduce heat to low and keep warm (discard any unopened clams).

In large pot of boiling, salted water, cook the pasta al dente, about 7 minutes. Drain the pasta, toss with clams and continue to cook, turning a few times, about 2 minutes. Add the fresh parsley, turn once, and serve.

Penne with Pesto Sauce

In a large pot, bring salted water to a boil, cook pasta for about 8 minutes (until al dente).

Place basil, pine-nuts, garlic, oil, and half the grated cheese into food processor, pulse several times, and blend well for ten seconds.

Heat pesto sauce (not too hot), toss with pasta and remainder of grated cheese, and serve.

Garnish with a few fresh basil leaves.

1 pound penne rigate (Barilla brand if available)
2 cups fresh basil
½ cup lightly toasted pine nuts
¾ cup extra virgin olive oil
¼ cup grated parmesan cheese
2 cloves garlic crushed

Primavera Pasta Salad

- **¾ pound tricolor fusilli pasta**
- **¾ pound tricolor cheese tortellini**
- **3 bell peppers: 1 red, 1 green, 1 yellow**
- **2 medium carrots, julienned**
- **3 scallions, cut in small rings**
- **1 small red onion, minced**
- **1 tablespoon chopped fresh parsley**
- **¼ cup pitted black olives, cut in half**
- **1 cup broccoli florets, blanched and quick-chilled**
- **⅓ cup Italian salad dressing**
- **Kosher salt and pepper to taste**

Cook pasta according to package directions, about 7–8 minutes.

Rinse under cold water to stop the cooking process.

Toss pasta with the dressing and other ingredients, taste for seasoning, and serve.

Serves 8.

Risotto Four Cheese

In a hot pot, melt butter, add onions and cook until soft, about 3–4 minutes. Add rice, stir constantly for ½ minute or so, just to absorb the liquid. Add wine and keep stirring as the liquid is being absorbed to prevent the rice from sticking, and add chicken stock as needed. The rice should be cooked in about 25 minutes.

When the rice is done, take off the fire, add gruyére, fontina, gorgonzola and parmesan, toss well, and serve.

Garnish with fresh parsley.

Could be served as main dish, or as a side order.

3–4 tablespoons butter
1 medium onion, finely chopped
4–5 cups simmering chicken stock
2 cups Arborio rice
1 cup dry white wine
½ cup grated gruyére cheese
½ cup finely diced fontina cheese
¾ cup grated parmesan cheese
½ cup gorgonzola cheese, finely crumbled
salt and pepper to taste

Risotto Parmigiano

5-6 cups chicken stock
1 tablespoon olive oil
1 onion, minced
1½ cups Arborio rice
3 tablespoons butter, softened
2 cloves minced garlic
2 tablespoons chopped Italian parsley
½ cup parmesan cheese
salt and pepper to taste

In a saucepan bring the stock to a simmer.

In a separate saucepan, sauté the onion on medium heat, stirring until the onion is soft but not brown. Add the minced garlic to the onion, and stir for about 10 seconds, then stir in the rice long enough to absorb some of the oil.

Add the simmering chicken stock to the pan with the onion and rice, about one cup at a time, as the rice absorbs it. Keep stirring frequently or it will stick to the pan. It may take 25–30 minutes for all the stock to be absorbed, so add more as needed until the rice reaches the desired tenderness.

When the rice is done, stir in the butter and cheese, sprinkle with parsley and black pepper, and serve.

Shredded Coconut Rice

1 cup long grain rice, rinsed
1¼ cups coconut milk
1 cup chicken stock
2 tablespoons sliced almonds
1 cup frozen peas
1 tablespoon finely sliced scallions
salt to taste

Bring coconut milk, chicken stock, and salt to a boil. Add the rice and cook for about 8–10 minutes. Add peas, shredded coconut, and scallion, and simmer for a few minutes more. Stir occasionally, adding water if needed. When the rice is tender and the liquid is absorbed, it is ready to serve.

TIP: Can be served as main dish, or as a side order.

Spaghetti with Garlic and Oil

1 pound spaghetti
6–7 tablespoons extra virgin olive oil
3–4 cloves garlic, peeled, crushed, and minced
4 tablespoons chopped fresh parsley
salt and pepper to taste
fresh grated parmesan cheese
1 tablespoon plain bread crumbs
pinch of crushed red hot pepper (optional)

Cook spaghetti in a large pot of rapidly boiling, salted water, 8 minutes (until al dente) and drain.

In a frying pan heat the oil gently, and sauté the garlic until it is barely golden (don't let it brown). Stir in the parsley, hot pepper, and bread crumbs. Add the pasta and turn until all the liquid is absorbed, toss for 1–2 minutes, then add the grated cheese and serve.

TIP: Toss in a small amount of toasted pine nuts for a unique and flavorful addition.

Vegetables

ST VLADIMIR'S ORTHODOX THEOLOGICAL SEMINARY
IC XC
1938 2013

Curried Vegetables

1 onion, peeled and chopped
3 tablespoons extra virgin olive oil
1 clove garlic, peeled and minced
1 pound cauliflower florets
1 medium eggplant, cut into 1-inch cubes, skin on
1 cup fresh chopped tomatoes
1 cup water
½ cup white wine
4–5 carrots, peeled and cut into ¼-inch rounds
½ pound green peas, fresh or frozen
2 cups white potatoes, peeled and chopped
1½ tablespoons curry powder
½ teaspoon cardamom
¼ teaspoon cayenne pepper
2 bay leaves
2 tablespoons fresh chopped parsley
salt and pepper to taste

In a large pot, heat oil, and sauté onion for 2 minutes; add garlic and stir, then add all the liquids and bring to a boil. Add all of the seasonings, then all of the vegetables except the parsley. Mix, cover, and simmer for 20–25 minutes on medium-low heat, turning a few times and tasting for seasoning. Adjust with salt and pepper. The vegetables are done when they are soft. Take out bay leaves and discard; add parsley, and stir.

Serve hot with basmati rice.

TIP: Can be served as a main dish or as a side.

Red Lentil Curry

2 cups red lentils
1 onion, chopped
1 tablespoon olive oil
2 tablespoons curry paste
1 tablespoon curry powder
1 teaspoon turmeric
1 teaspoon cumin
1 teaspoon chili powder
1 tablespoon sugar
1 teaspoon fresh chopped garlic
1 teaspoon fresh chopped ginger
1½ cups tomato purée
salt and pepper to taste

Rinse the lentils well, cover with water, and simmer until tender. Add more hot water if needed. In the meantime, start caramelizing the onion in oil.

Mix well the remaining ingredients and bring them to a simmer for about 2–3 minutes. Add them to the cooked onion and continue to simmer for a few more minutes. Drain the lentils, add them to the curry base, toss, and serve.

Serves 6.

Eggplant Parmigiana

3–4 medium size eggplants
2 cups all-purpose flour
2 cups seasoned bread crumbs
6 –7 eggs, lightly beaten
3 cups of your favorite tomato sauce
2 cups shredded mozzarella
2 tablespoons grated parmesan cheese
1 tablespoon minced parsley
1½ cups vegetable oil for frying

Take half the peel off the eggplants by peeling alternate slices lengthwise (black and white stripes); cut the both ends off, then slice them lengthwise about ¼-inch thick.

In one working dish place the flour; in another working dish, the bread crumbs; and in another, the eggs. Take one slice of eggplant at a time, dredge it in flour, shake off the excess, dip the piece into the eggs, shake off the excess, and then cover the eggplant with bread crumbs on both sides. With the palm of your hand press down on both sides so the bread crumbs stay in place.

In a frying pan, heat the oil to 375F, then take the breaded eggplant and start frying in small batches, turning once, until light golden brown. Take each slice out of the oil and place on a dry paper towel.

Preheat the oven to 375F.

Cover the bottom of an 8×10 baking pan with tomato sauce. Add one layer of the fried eggplant. Drizzle some tomato sauce over that, cover with 1/3 of the mozzarella, repeat for the next two layers, and top off with the rest of the tomato sauce, mozzarella, grated cheese, and parsley.

Cover the dish and bake for 15 minutes; then uncover and keep cooking for an additional 15–20 minutes, or until hot. Let it cool for 7–10 minutes, cut it into square portions, and serve.

French-fried Eggplant

1 medium eggplant, peeled and cut in sticks (like potatoes)
water
salt and pepper to taste
paprika to taste
½ cup cornmeal
¼ cup all-purpose flour
½ teaspoon white pepper
¼ teaspoon cornstarch
vegetable oil for frying

Place the eggplant sticks in ice cold salted water and set aside for 20 minutes.

Mix together paprika, cornmeal, flour, white pepper, cornstarch, and salt to taste.

Drain eggplant; dredge in the cornmeal mixture, making sure the pieces are well coated. Fry in hot oil in small batches; with slotted spoon remove and place on dry paper towels.

TIP: Zucchini squash works just as well for this recipe.

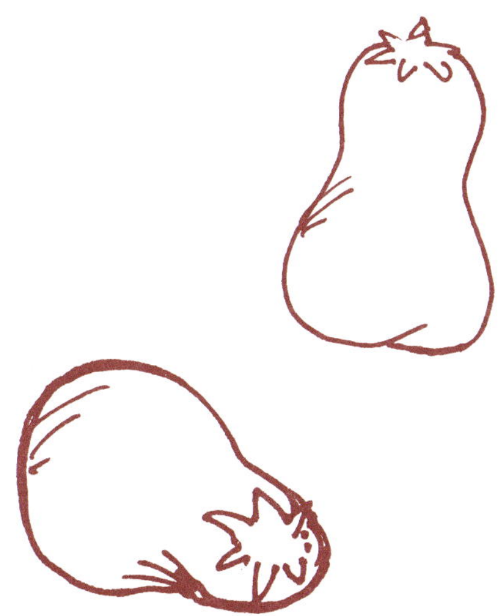

Mediterranean Vegetable Stew

3 tablespoons extra virgin olive oil
1 cup chopped onion
2 cups red and green bell pepper
3 cloves garlic, peeled and chopped
1 cup sliced mushrooms
1 medium eggplant, washed and cut in 1-inch chunks
1 yellow zucchini, washed and cut in 1-inch chunks
1 green squash, washed and cut in 1-inch chunks
½ cup white wine
1 28-ounce can crushed tomatoes
½ cup kalamata olives, pitted and sliced in half
1 15-ounce can chickpeas, drained and rinsed
1 teaspoon chopped fresh rosemary
salt and pepper to taste
½ cup chopped fresh parsley
1 cup vegetable stock or chicken stock, if needed to make "soupier," but plain water will do just fine

In a large pot, heat the oil and cook the onions for 5–6 minutes until soft, then add the garlic. Cook for 30 seconds and add the bell peppers; cook and turn 2 minutes, then add mushrooms, eggplant, zucchini, squash, wine, crushed tomatoes, olives, chickpeas, rosemary, salt, and pepper. Stir until vegetables are somewhat soft but not mushy, about 15 minutes. Toss with fresh parsley and serve hot.

Scalloped Potatoes

6–8 potatoes, thinly sliced (1/8-inch)
2 onions, thinly sliced
2 tablespoons butter for greasing pan
3/4 cup seasoned bread crumbs
2 cups heavy cream
1/4 cup grated parmesan cheese
salt and pepper to taste

Grease a baking pan with butter.

Preheat oven to 400F.

Drizzle some heavy cream in base of pan, then build layers of:

potatoes

onions

cheese

bread crumbs

salt and pepper

Continue the process until pan is filled, then top with heavy cream and bread crumbs, bake, covered, for 30 minutes. Uncover and bake until the top is browned and the potatoes are tender.

Serbian Prebranac (Lima Beans)

2 pounds dry lima beans
2 pounds large onions
1 pound bacon, cut in small pieces
½ cup vegetable oil
1 teaspoon paprika
1 teaspoon cayenne pepper
3 bay leaves
salt and pepper to taste

Preheat oven to 400F.

Soak lima beans overnight in salted cold water.

Peel and slice onions. Boil the lima beans in the salted water (add water if needed) until tender, but not too soft. Set aside.

Sauté onions and bacon until onions are caramelized and bacon is cooked; add paprika, cayenne pepper, bay leaves.

In a greased baking pan, layer the beans and the onion mixture, repeating the process until the ingredients are used up; the top layer must be onion mixture.

Bake for up to 35–40 minutes, or until golden brown.

TIP: Add extra crushed red pepper if desired.

Stuffed Mushrooms

Preheat oven to 400F.

In a frying pan, heat the oil and butter; sauté the onions and mushroom stems, about 2–3 minutes, then add the bread crumbs and the rest of seasonings. Toss well to combine and add additional oil if needed to make moister. Place the stuffing into the mushroom cavity, and bake for about 10 minutes.

Serve hot; garnish with sprig of fresh parsley or a lemon wedge.

12 large white mushrooms, washed (cut off the stems and dice them)
1 tablespoon olive oil
1 tablespoon butter
pinch of thyme
1 tablespoon chopped fresh parsley
3 tablespoons minced onion
1½ cups bread crumbs (seasoned)
1 tablespoon grated parmesan cheese
pinch black pepper

Stuffed Zucchini Logs

4 medium sized zucchini
1 small onion, peeled and chopped
2 cloves garlic, peeled and minced
¼ cup mushrooms, minced
1 tablespoon olive oil
2 tablespoons butter
1 ounce white wine
1 tablespoon all-purpose flour
½ cup red and green bell peppers, finely chopped
½ cup shredded monterey jack cheese and cheddar cheese (mix)
¼ cup grated parmesan cheese
¼ cup seasoned bread crumbs
1 tablespoon chopped fresh parsley
pinch of salt, pepper, oregano to taste

Preheat oven to 400F.

Bring a small pot of lightly salted water to boil; blanch the zucchini for 6–7 minutes.

Drain the zucchini and cut about ½ inch off the ends, core the insides to create empty zucchini tubes and set aside, leaving some of the white pulp and skin intact.

In a skillet, heat the oil and butter; sauté onion and garlic, then add mushrooms and peppers. Add wine and cook and stir for 2–3 minutes, until vegetables are soft. Add flour, bread crumbs, and cheeses, while continually stirring to get a good mixture. Mix in parsley and seasoning. Let cool for a few minutes then stuff mixture into the zucchini.

Place stuffed zucchini in a baking pan and bake for 8–10 minutes.

TIP: If there's any stuffing left over, save for stuffed mushrooms.

Tabouli

Cover the bulgur with boiling water for 1 hour to soften. If not soft enough, drain and repeat process for half hour. When ready, mix well with all ingredients and seasonings, chill for a few hours, and serve.

TIP: Great as a salad!

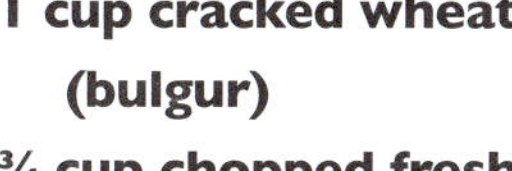

1 cup cracked wheat (bulgur)
¾ cup chopped fresh parsley
1 green onion, thinly sliced
½ cup extra virgin olive oil
½ cup fresh-squeezed lemon juice
1 cucumber, seeded and finely chopped
3 plum tomatoes, seeded and finely chopped
1 tablespoon chopped mint leaves
½ teaspoon minced garlic
Salt and pepper to taste

Two-Bean Puerto Rican Sofritos

½ pound red beans
½ pound white beans
⅓ cup sofrito (see below)
1 cup tomato sauce
2 teaspoons bacon drippings
salt and pepper to taste
water

For Sofrito

1 tablespoon olive oil
1 onion, finely chopped
3 chili peppers, seeded and finely chopped
2 cloves garlic, peeled and minced
1 green pepper, seeded and chopped
1 bunch cilantro, washed and chopped
½ teaspoon oregano

To make the sofrito, sauté the onion, chili, garlic, green pepper, cilantro, and oregano with oil and bacon drippings until soft, about 5–6 minutes. Add beans and tomato sauce, and top with water, but just enough to cover the beans. Season with salt and pepper to taste and bring to a boil; cook over medium heat until liquid starts to look like a sauce. Add more water if needed. Keep cooking until beans are soft but yet with a bite (not too soft!).

TIP: Serve either as a side or as a main dish.

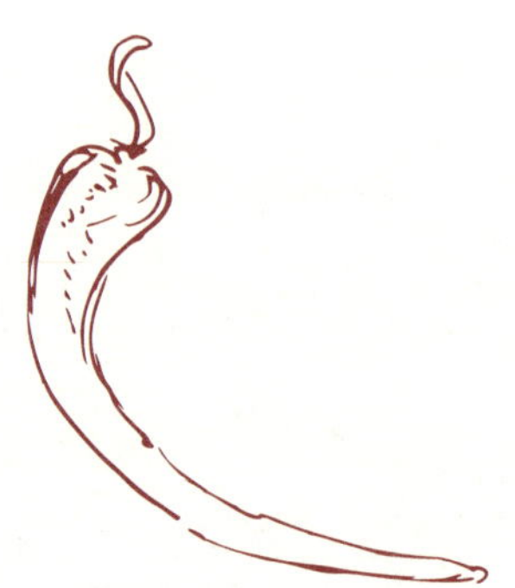

Meat

ST VLADIMIR'S ORTHODOX
IC XC
1938 2013
THEOLOGICAL SEMINARY

Adobo Mexican Pork Chops

8 pork chops, bone in, 1-inch thick
3 tablespoons brown sugar
3 tablespoons olive oil
4 tablespoons freshly squeezed orange juice
2 tablespoons chopped fresh cilantro
¼ cup white wine
2 teaspoons chili powder
1 teaspoon ground cumin
1 teaspoon dried oregano
¼ teaspoon cayenne pepper
¼ teaspoon ground cinnamon
3 teaspoons minced fresh garlic
salt and pepper to taste

Place the pork chops in a container large enough so the marinade can be added to it.

To make the marinade, using a whisk, combine all the other ingredients in a mixing bowl. Add marinade to pork chops, rub into the meat, cover with plastic wrap, and refrigerate for 1 hour, turning meat a few times.

In the meantime, heat grill to about 500F, place the chops on a greased grill for about 6–7 minutes. Turn chops to a 45-degree angle to give them nice cross lines, cook for 6–7 minutes more, turn over the other side, and cook for additional 10–12 minutes, until fully cooked.

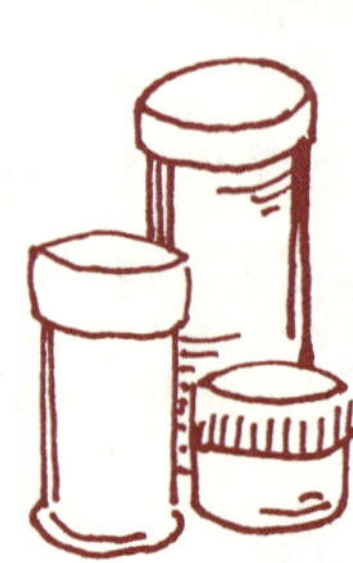

TIP: To grease the grill, just fold a paper napkin a few times, dip in oil, and, using tongs, wipe it across the hot grill, so the grilling product won't stick.

Bacon-Wrapped Bratwursts

5 bratwursts
5 cups beer
4 tablespoons brown sugar
1 teaspoon chili powder
½ teaspoon cayenne pepper
15 slices lean bacon

Bring the beer to a simmer; poke the bratwursts with a toothpick or a fork a few times. Place them in the simmering beer and cook for about 18–20 minutes.

Remove the bratwursts; let them cool to room temperature.

Preheat oven to 450F.

Cut bratwursts into thirds and set aside.

Mix together brown sugar, chili powder, and cayenne. Toss the bratwursts in the mixture to get a nice coating, and then wrap each piece with one strip of bacon and secure it with a toothpick to hold the two together.

Line them up on a sheet pan and bake about 25–30 minutes or until bacon is nice and brown. Shake the pan a few times to prevent meat from sticking and to allow meat to be evenly cooked.

Baked Chicken and Pomodoro (Tomatoes)

4 boneless breasts of chicken
½ teaspoon dried basil
½ teaspoon dried parsley
½ teaspoon crushed red pepper
½ teaspoon dried oregano
salt and pepper to taste
1 ½ tablespoons extra virgin olive oil
8 slices beefsteak tomato

Preheat oven to 350F.

Mix together oil, basil, parsley, red pepper, oregano, and salt and pepper.

Rub the mixture evenly onto each chicken breast; set aside.

Grease a baking pan, place chicken on bottom of pan, top each breast with 2 slices of tomatoes, cover with aluminum foil, and bake for 20–25 minutes, then uncover and keep cooking for additional 15–17 minutes until the surface starts to brown and the chicken is fully cooked.

Garnish with fresh basil leaves.

Serve with roasted potatoes.

Baked Pork Chops

6 thin pork cops
3 eggs, beaten
½ teaspoon garlic powder
½ teaspoon onion powder
¾ cup seasoned bread crumbs
4 tablespoons vegetable oil for frying
1 teaspoon butter
salt and pepper to taste

Preheat oven to 375F.

In a shallow bowl, thoroughly blend bread crumbs, garlic powder, and onion powder.

Beat the eggs in a separate bowl; season them with a pinch of salt and pepper.

Dip the pork chops into the egg mixture; press down into bread crumbs on all sides.

Preheat oil and the butter in skillet; fry the meat 3 minutes on each side until light brown and crispy. Transfer to baking a pan and cook in the preheated oven for 35–40 minutes or until fully cooked (no pink on the inside).

Serve hot and garnish with lemon wedges.

TIP: Excellent with garlic mashed potatoes and sautéed spinach.

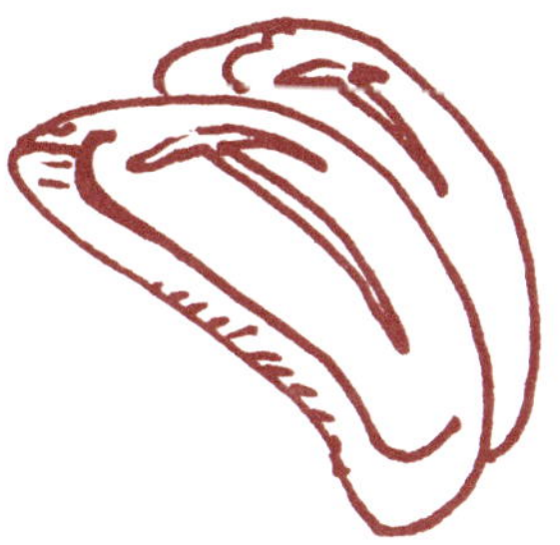

BBQ Bratwursts

6 fresh bratwursts
Your favorite BBQ sauce

Preheat grill to high.

Split open bratwursts lengthwise, place them on the grill, brush them with BBQ sauce on both sides, turning once or twice, until done, about 12–14 minutes; serve on club rolls or buns.

BBQ Coffee-Flavored Beef

Mix all the ingredients except the meat to form a marinade, pour it over the meat, and marinate the meat overnight in the refrigerator, turning once or twice.

Preheat grill and place meat on the grill. Brush some of the marinade over the meat and save the rest. Reduce heat to low, close the lid, and keep cooking about 20–25 minutes. Turn the meat and brush with more marinade; after 15–20 minutes check to see if it's done.

Cook the remainder of marinade to make a sauce, and keep warm. Carve meat in thin slices across the grain, and layer on a serving platter. Drizzle hot marinade sauce on top, and serve.

1 3-4 pound beef roast
1 cup ketchup
½ cup water
¼ cup white vinegar
¼ cup olive oil
4 tablespoons instant coffee
1 teaspoon chili powder
1 teaspoon celery seeds
½ teaspoon fresh garlic, minced
¼ teaspoon Tabasco sauce (optional)
1 bay leaf
Salt and pepper to taste

Beef Stir-Fry

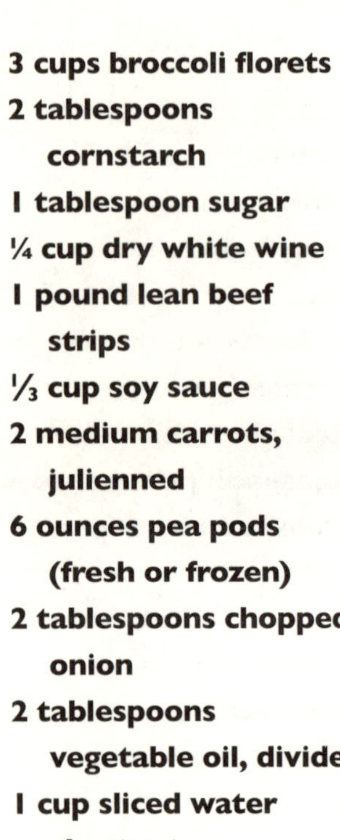

3 cups broccoli florets
2 tablespoons cornstarch
1 tablespoon sugar
¼ cup dry white wine
1 pound lean beef strips
⅓ cup soy sauce
2 medium carrots, julienned
6 ounces pea pods (fresh or frozen)
2 tablespoons chopped onion
2 tablespoons vegetable oil, divided
1 cup sliced water chestnuts (one 8-ounce can works well)
salt and pepper to taste

Whisk together cornstarch, sugar, wine, and soy sauce until smooth. Add the beef and toss to coat well and set aside. In a large skillet, heat oil for 30 seconds; stir-fry broccoli, carrots, pea pods, and onion for 1 minute, then add water chestnuts, cover, and simmer on low heat for 3–4 minutes.

Remove from heat and set aside. In the same skillet, stir-fry beef with the remaining oil until done. Return vegetables to the skillet, toss well, and serve.

Taste for seasoning, add salt and pepper if needed.

TIP: Delicious with steamed rice.

Beef Stroganoff

In a hot skillet, heat oil and butter. Toss beef in the flour, then cook the beef in hot butter and oil, searing on all sides. Take out the beef and set aside; sauté onions in the same butter and oil, then add mushrooms, beef stock, tomato paste, and sour cream. Add beef back into the skillet and keep cooking for additional 15–20 minutes, until meat is tender. Season with salt and pepper.

Adjust the thickness of sauce with cornstarch if necessary.

Serve with steamed rice.

Serves 4.

2 pounds cubed beef tenderloin
1 pound fresh mushrooms, sliced in half
¾ cup sour cream
1½ cups beef stock
2 onions, chopped
2–3 tablespoons tomato paste
3 tablespoons flour
3 tablespoons butter
2 tablespoons vegetable oil
Salt and pepper to taste

Blackened Filet Mignon

4 6-ounce pieces of filet mignon
About 3–4 tablespoons coarse black pepper
2 tablespoons olive oil
Kosher salt to taste

Season filets generously on all sides with black pepper and a little salt, to taste, and set aside for a few minutes.

Heat oil in hot skillet, sear the filets on all sides, and cook to desired doneness.

Serve with portabella mushrooms sautéed in the same skillet.

Serves 4.

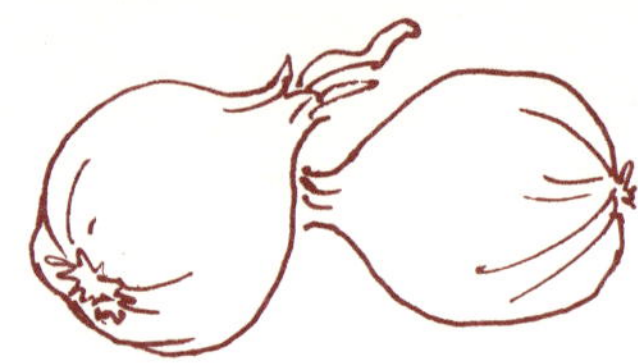

Brined Bratwursts

8 fresh bratwursts
¾ cup balsamic vinegar
2 onions, sliced
2 cups water
3 cups beer
2 teaspoons butter

In a pot, start simmering water, beer, onions, and balsamic vinegar. Simmer for 12–15 minutes and then place the bratwursts in the simmering liquid; simmer for 20–25 minutes more.

Preheat grill on high.

Remove bratwursts from pot and set aside. Drain liquid; add butter to the onions and cook until brown, then place bratwursts on the grill, turning until browned on all sides.

Serve with the onions.

Serves 8.

Chicken Al Vesuvio

2 pounds chicken breasts and thighs
4 tablespoons olive oil for frying
1¾ pounds small red potatoes, peeled and cut in half
3 large cloves garlic, peeled, crushed, and minced
¾ cup white wine
¾ cup chicken broth
1 teaspoon dried oregano
1 teaspoon dried thyme
12-ounce jar artichoke hearts (with half of the liquid)
2 tablespoons butter
salt and pepper to taste
1 tablespoon fresh chopped parsley

Preheat oven to 450F.

Heat the oil in an ovenproof pot.

Season the chicken with salt and pepper, and cook in the hot oil, turning as necessary, until golden brown on all sides, about 10-Minutes. Transfer the chicken to a bowl; then add the potatoes to the pot; cook them until they start to brown, stirring occasionally, for about 10–12 minutes.

Add the garlic and sauté for 1 minute, then add the wine and quickly stir to deglaze the bottom of the pot. Add the broth, oregano, and the thyme, and return the chicken to the pot; stir to combine, bringing the liquid to a boil over medium-high heat.

Cover and cook in the oven for about 20 minutes.

Arrange the chicken and potatoes on a serving platter, then add the artichoke hearts to the sauce and simmer for a few minutes. Add the butter and simmer for a few minutes more, until the artichoke hearts are tender. Pour the sauce over the potatoes and the chicken and serve.

Garnish with fresh chopped parsley.

TIP: 2 tablespoons of pitted black olives cut in half can be added for color and taste.

Chicken and Shrimp Piedmontese

10 chicken thighs on the bone, with skin off
10 large shrimp, cleaned and deveined
10 large shrimp with shells on
½ cup extra virgin olive oil
1½ cups onion, finely chopped
1 celery stalk, finely chopped
2 cloves garlic, mashed and minced
14 ounces plum tomatoes, peeled, seeded, chopped
1 cup dry white wine
1 teaspoon fresh rosemary, finely chopped
1 tablespoon butter
10 triangles of sliced Italian bread
2 tablespoons fresh chopped parsley
pinch of crushed red pepper
salt and pepper to taste

In a frying pan, heat 2–3 tablespoons of oil and sauté the chicken on medium heat until it starts to brown, turning frequently. After 6–7 minutes, transfer the chicken to a deep casserole dish and set aside.

In the frying pan, cook the onions and celery, gently turning for two minutes, until soft; add the garlic, tomatoes, wine, rosemary, some salt and pepper, and a pinch of hot pepper. Bring to a boil and cook for 3 minutes more.

Pour the tomato sauce over the chicken, cover, and cook for about 35–40 minutes or until the chicken is done and tender.

Add all the shrimp to the tomato sauce along with the chicken, and keep cooking for 5–6 minutes more, or until all the shrimp is fully cooked and red-pink.

In a frying pan, heat the remainder of the oil and butter, brown the bread on both sides, and set aside.

TIP: This dish can be served family style on a large serving platter, with toasted bread on top inner rim of the platter; or divide equally into five portions and serve.

Garnish with fresh parsley

Chicken Piccata

6 chicken cutlets, skinless, boneless, and pounded
½ cup flour
salt and white pepper to taste
½ teaspoon paprika
1 egg
3 tablespoons milk
2 tablespoons butter
2 tablespoons olive oil
½ pound mushrooms, rinsed and sliced
½ cup chicken stock
½ cup white wine
2 tablespoons lemon juice
1 teaspoon cornstarch
1 teaspoon capers
1 tablespoon fresh chopped parsley for garnish

Mix together flour, salt, white pepper, and paprika; set aside.

Mix egg and milk; set aside.

In a skillet, heat the butter and oil.

Dip chicken in egg mix then in flour mix; shake off the excess, then place in the hot skillet.

Lightly brown cutlets on both sides, then remove them to a plate lined with paper towels. In the same skillet, sauté mushrooms for 3–4 minutes, then add the chicken stock, white wine, lemon juice, and cornstarch. Bring the mixture to a boil, and then simmer for 2 minutes until the sauce starts to thicken a little. Place the chicken back in the skillet, add the capers, and continue to simmer until all is fully cooked and the sauce is the right consistency.

Garnish with parsley and sliced lemon.

Serves 6.

TIP: This dish works well served with broccoli cooked with oil and garlic.

Chicken Quesadilla

2 flour tortillas
½ cup Mexican cheese
1 chicken breast

Spray large pan with grease and warm it up; grill and slice chicken breast.

Place flour tortilla on pan and spread cheese on it.

Quickly add chicken and place second tortilla over it.

Carefully flip several times. It is done when all the cheese is melted and the tortillas are light brown.

Easy Baked Chicken

8 boneless and skinless chicken breasts
1 cup bread crumbs
1 cup mayonnaise
½ cup parmesan cheese
¼ teaspoon granulated garlic
¼ teaspoon dried oregano
¼ teaspoon dried basil
salt and pepper to taste

Preheat oven to 400F.

In a bowl, mix together the mayonnaise, grated cheese, garlic, oregano, basil, and salt and pepper. Coat the chicken well with the mayonnaise mixture, then put the breasts into the bread crumbs to get an even coating. Place the chicken in a lightly greased baking pan and bake for about 25 minutes or so, or until chicken is fully cooked.

Chicken Parmesan

Preheat oven to 375F.

Whisk eggs in a medium bowl. Place bread crumbs on shallow plate and the flour on a second shallow plate. Coat each cutlet with flour, shake off the excess; then coat with eggs, shake off the excess; then coat well with bread crumbs, and pat down with the palm of your hand.

In a hot skillet, heat the oil and the butter to about 400F. Fry all 4 cutlets for 4–5 minutes on each side until fully cooked (no pink on the inside). Transfer the cutlets to a paper towel.

Heat tomato sauce, place half of it in a baking pan large enough for all 4 cutlets.

Spread the cutlets flat and top them with remainder of the sauce. Then cover each cutlet with mozzarella and grated cheese, and bake for about 10 minutes. Garnish with fresh chopped parsley.

Serve with a side of spaghetti and the same sauce.

Serves 4.

4–6 ounces of chicken cutlets
4 tablespoons vegetable oil
1 tablespoon butter
¾ cup seasoned bread crumbs
½ cup all-purpose flour
2 large eggs, beaten
4 teaspoons grated parmesan cheese
1 tablespoon fresh chopped parsley
10 ounces Italian marinara sauce
¾ cup shredded mozzarella

Feta Cheese Chicken

6 boneless chicken breasts (lightly pounded to tenderize)
4 tablespoons balsamic vinaigrette
2 teaspoons Italian seasoning
salt and pepper to taste
12 slices plum tomatoes
1 cup crumbled feta cheese

Preheat oven to 375F.

Brush each chicken breast with vinaigrette and sprinkle with seasoning.

In a hot, ovenproof skillet, sear both sides of chicken until cooked. Top each breast with two slices of tomatoes and divide feta cheese on top of tomatoes. (If you do not have an ovenproof skillet, transfer the chicken to a baking pan before adding the tomatoes.)

Bake until the cheese starts to brown.

Serves 6.

German Pork Loin and Sauerkraut

Preheat oven to 350F.

Mix together sauerkraut, apples, onions, brown sugar, and caraway seeds; set aside.

Rub the pieces of pork loin with half the oil, and put the rest of the oil in the skillet. Sear the meat on all sides until brown. Place them in a baking pan and top with the mixture; cover with aluminum foil and bake for about 40–45 minutes or until the meat is well done and really tender. Drain some of the liquid, and serve.

TIP: Pork chops work well also. Serve with German roasted potatoes.

Serves 6.

6 portions of pork loin, 6–7 ounces each
3 tablespoons olive oil
1½ pounds sauerkraut with juice
2 red apples, cored, peeled, and sliced
1 onion, peeled and thinly sliced
½ cup brown sugar
2 teaspoons caraway seeds

Ginger Pork Loin

2 pounds pork loin, trimmed
2 tablespoons olive oil
2 tablespoons butter
2 tablespoons soy sauce
1 tablespoon sesame oil
1 tablespoon hoi sin sauce
1½ teaspoons fresh grated ginger
½ teaspoon crushed and chopped garlic
½ teaspoon oregano
1 teaspoon fresh parsley
¼ cup white wine
salt and pepper to taste

Place the pork loin in a freezer for one hour (this makes it easier to slice).

Using a sharp knife, slice the pork loin into thin round slices about ⅛-inch thick, then cut the slices into quarter-inch strips.

Heat oil in a skillet and add butter. Sauté garlic for one minute, add the pork strips, and cook for 10–12 minutes until almost done. Add soy sauce, sesame oil, and hoi sin sauce.

Add oregano, fresh ginger, and wine.

Simmer for 3–4 minutes until the wine reduces a little, turning frequently.

Bring the flame to low-medium, and simmer for an additional 10 minutes, or until meat is fully cooked. Season with salt and pepper and serve.

TIP: This goes well with rice and broccoli.

Grilled Chicken Paillard

6 boneless, skinless chicken breasts, pounded to tenderize
½ cup fresh lemon juice
1 small shallot, peeled and minced
¼ cup extra virgin olive oil
Salt and pepper to taste

FOR THE SALAD

1 pound arugula
18 ripe cherry tomatoes
1 large red onion, peeled, cut in half, and thinly sliced
3 tablespoons balsamic vinegar
3 tablespoons extra virgin olive oil, plus some for drizzling
salt and pepper to taste
6 wedges of lemon for garnish

Whisk together lemon juice, shallots, oil, salt and pepper; marinate chicken in liquid for about 30 minutes in refrigerator.

Heat grill to high, remove the chicken from marinade, and grill for 2–3 minutes on each side, or until cooked through.

Whisk together balsamic vinegar, oil, salt, and pepper, and toss with arugula, cherry tomatoes, and sliced onion. Arrange on a serving platter, then place the chicken evenly over the salad, with the lemon wedges around the edge. Drizzle with olive oil.

TIP: This dish is delicious with thin-cut French fries.

Hawaiian Beef Skewers

2 pounds beef sirloin, cut into bite-size pieces
2 tablespoons fresh ginger strips
2 cloves of garlic, mashed
1 onion, chopped
1 cup soy sauce
4 tablespoons sugar
6 small hot dried chili peppers
2 tablespoons red wine vinegar
4 teaspoons cornstarch
½ cup water at room temperature

In a small pan, combine ginger, garlic, onion, soy sauce, sugar, hot peppers, and vinegar.

Cook over medium heat, about 20–25 minutes. In a separate small bowl, dissolve cornstarch in water, and then slowly pour it into the sauce, stirring continuously, until somewhat thick (not too thick). Cook a few minutes, then pour into a bowl through a fine wire strainer; discard the pulp.

Let the sauce cool, mix the beef with the sauce and marinate for 1–2 hours.

Thread 4 pieces of meat on each skewer; barbecue over hot grill (or broil) until cooked, and serve.

Jamaican Fried Chicken

Rinse the chicken pieces well and pat them dry with a paper towel. Combine chicken, salt and pepper, dried thyme, and onions. Marinate in refrigerator about one hour.

Place bread crumbs in a bowl large enough to work the chicken.

In a different bowl, beat the eggs; dip each piece of chicken into the egg mixture until well coated. Then roll each piece in the bread crumbs until well coated.

Preheat oil in a large skillet (or do two batches if your skillet is not large enough to accommodate all the chicken at once).

Place the chicken in hot oil and cook for about 35–40 minutes on medium heat.

Turn each piece a few times for an even, crispy crust.

Serve with French fries.

8–10 pieces of chicken parts (breasts and legs)
salt and pepper to taste
2 teaspoons dried thyme
2 onions, sliced
3 cups plain bread crumbs
2–3 eggs
½ cup vegetable oil

Lamb Stew

3 pounds lamb, cut in cubes
3 tablespoons butter
2 tablespoons olive oil
3 tablespoons flour
1 large carrot, peeled and cut in chunks
1 large onion, peeled and chopped
2 large potatoes, peeled and cut in large chunks
1 green squash, cleaned and cut in quarters lengthwise, seeded, and chopped
1 yellow squash, cleaned and cut (same as green squash)
½ pound green beans, washed and cut in half
2 cloves garlic, peeled and minced
2 beefsteak tomatoes, chopped
pinch dried oregano
pinch dried basil
salt and pepper, to taste
hot crushed red pepper, to taste
1 cup red wine
10 ounces tomato sauce
1 tablespoon chopped fresh parsley

In a hot skillet, heat oil and butter. Toss meat in the flour and then sear the meat in hot oil on all sides. Season the vegetables with the oregano, basil, salt, pepper and red pepper. Add wine and the seasoned vegetables.

Add tomato sauce and cover; cook for 35–40 minutes, stirring occasionally.

When the meat and vegetables are nice and tender, the dish can be served with or without rice.

Toss with fresh parsley before serving.

Serves 6.

Mango Chicken

In a hot skillet, heat oil and butter, and cook onion. Add garlic and cook until onions are tender, then add chicken. Cook about one minute while stirring; stir in curry paste, making sure the chicken is thoroughly coated. Pour in the chutney and tomatoes; keep cooking until the chicken is done—about 12–15 minutes—and serve.

Serves 6.

1 teaspoon butter

1 tablespoon olive oil

2–3 cloves fresh garlic, finely minced

2–2½ pounds boneless chicken breast, cut in bite-sized pieces

3 tablespoons curry paste

¾ cup mango chutney

1 28-ounce can diced tomatoes, drained

Mexican Pizza

6 corn tortillas
16 ounces refried beans
1 pound ground beef
1 tablespoon taco seasoning mix
2 tablespoons vegetable oil
1 pound cheddar cheese, shredded
¾ cup sour cream
3 plum tomatoes, chopped
3 green onions, chopped
¼ cup diced green chili peppers, drained
1 peeled avocado, pitted and diced
2 tablespoons black olives, pitted and sliced

Preheat oven to 350F.

Heat refried beans.

In a skillet, brown the beef and add the taco seasoning; remove the meat. Add a little oil and heat the tortillas one at a time.

Place tortillas on a sheet pan, spread refried beans on each tortilla, followed by beef and cheese, then bake for 15–18 minutes, or until heated through and the cheese is melted.

Arrange on plates or serving platters, top them with the remaining ingredients, and serve.

TIP: This recipe makes either one large serving; or the pizza can be sliced into wedges for individual appetizers.

Open-Face Dripping Roast Beef

Preheat oven to 400F, or grill to high.

Split open the club rolls and set them on a baking pan.

In a sauce pan heat onion soup, Worcestershire sauce, and Tabasco for about 3 minutes. Place roast beef in hot sauce just to heat through (1 minute) and divide dripping roast beef among the rolls. Top each with overlapping slices of cheese.

Place in oven until the bread is slightly toasted, and the cheese melted, about 3 minutes.

Add a little more juice if you like, sprinkle parsley on top, and serve.

TIP: Serve with kosher pickles and French fries on the side.

Serves 4.

1 pound sliced deli roast beef
4 club rolls
1 small can French onion soup
1 tablespoon Worcestershire sauce
dash of Tabasco sauce (optional)
4 slices swiss cheese
4 slices provolone cheese
1 tablespoon chopped fresh parsley

Oven-Baked Chicken with Potatoes

2–3 pounds chicken parts (breasts, legs)
2 cloves garlic, peeled and mashed
2 tablespoons extra virgin olive oil
1 teaspoon oregano
1 teaspoon roasted garlic pepper
½ teaspoon dried basil
½ teaspoon dried parsley
1 small onion, chopped
½ cup white wine
salt and pepper to taste
2 pounds new red potatoes, cut in half (no need to peel)

Preheat oven to 450F.

Rinse chicken well, toss it with all the seasonings plus the oil and the wine.

Arrange the chicken in a baking dish big enough to add the potatoes later, and bake for about 35–40 minutes. Lower the temperature to 350F and add the potatoes. Mix together with chicken and continue baking, turning frequently, until chicken is fully cooked and potatoes are soft.

Pineapple Salsa Pork Tenderloin

Preheat oven to 425F.

Mix together brown sugar, ginger, mustard, chili powder, and cilantro; add a little salt and pepper. Rub the mixture onto the tenderloin and place it in a greased baking pan. Bake for about 40 minutes, or until the internal temperature reads 160F.

In the meantime, prepare the salsa and toss it together with all the other ingredients, season with salt and pepper to taste. Serve with tenderloin.

Garnish with a wedge of lemon and a sprig of fresh cilantro.

TIP: Serve with roasted red potatoes cooked with garlic and rosemary.

Serves 4.

2 pork tenderloins, 1 pound each
2½ tablespoons brown sugar
½ teaspoon fresh ginger, minced
salt and pepper to taste
2 tablespoons mustard
¼ teaspoon chili powder
1 teaspoon cilantro, finely chopped

For the salsa

2 cups fresh pineapple, chopped in small pieces
½ cup red bell pepper, seeded and chopped into small pieces
1 jalapeño, seeded and finely chopped
2 tablespoons green onion, finely chopped
1 tablespoon fresh cilantro, finely chopped
1 tablespoon brown sugar
juice of half a lime and half a lemon
salt and pepper to taste

Polish Meatloaf

1½ pounds ground beef
½ pound ground pork
3 onions, peeled and sliced
¾ cup mushrooms, cleaned and sliced
1 cup cooked rice
2 cups sour cream
2 tablespoons flour
2 tablespoons butter
2 tablespoons vegetable oil
½ teaspoon capers
salt and pepper to taste

Preheat oven to 350F.

In a hot skillet, heat butter and sauté beef and pork together, season with salt and pepper. Once cooked, take the meat out and set aside. In the same skillet, brown the onions, mushrooms, and capers.

Remove the onion mixture and leave the liquid in the skillet. In the same skillet, add oil, sour cream, and flour to make the sauce.

In a well-greased baking pan, start with a layer of meat, then add a layer of rice, then a layer of the onion mixture, and repeat the process until all the ingredients are used up. Top with the sour cream sauce and bake 30–35 minutes, then take the meatloaf out of the oven. Let it rest for a few minutes, and serve.

Serves 4.

Pork and Chicken Banana Stew

½ cup flour
salt and pepper to taste
1½ pounds boneless pork, cubed
1½ pounds boneless chicken breast
3 tablespoons olive oil
1 large onion, sliced
2 celery stalks, cleaned and chopped
1 green bell pepper, cleaned and chopped
1 red bell pepper, cleaned and chopped
2 cloves garlic, peeled, crushed, and minced
2 scotch bonnet finely chopped
1 cup water
1 cup white wine
1 large cucumber, peeled, seeded, and diced
4 medium tomatoes, chopped
6 firm bananas, peeled and sliced

Combine flour, salt, and pepper in a bowl, dredge pork in the flour, shake off excess flour; heat oil in a hot skillet, cook pork, browning and turning often (cook in batches if necessary); do same for the chicken, and set aside.

Reduce heat to low-medium while the skillet is still hot, pour half the wine in the skillet to deglaze it, and with a wooden spoon or spatula, scrape the bottom of the pan (10–15 seconds).

Add onion, celery, bell peppers, garlic, and scotch bonnet; cook for 10 minutes. Return pork and chicken to the skillet; add water and the remainder of the wine. Bring to a boil, then simmer until the pork and the chicken are fully cooked and tender, about 40–45 minutes.

Add cucumbers and tomatoes; cook for 10–15 minutes more; add bananas and heat only until they are nice and hot.

Serve with rice and vegetable of your choice.

Sloppy Joe Meatloaf

2 small onions, minced
3 stalks celery, cleaned and minced
5–6 ounces tomato paste
1¼ envelopes Sloppy Joe seasoning mix
1½ cups plain bread crumbs
2 eggs, beaten
1½ pounds ground beef
7-8 slices bacon

Preheat oven to 400F.

In a bowl, mix together the onion, celery, tomato paste, Sloppy Joe mix, bread crumbs, and eggs. With your hands, work the mixture into the beef until well combined. Shape into a loaf, and place in baking pan lined with aluminum foil. Place the bacon across the top of the loaf.

Bake for 30–35 minutes, then bring the heat down to 350F. Bake for additional 30–35 minutes or until fully cooked (spoon out most of the fat during the cooking process).

Let the meatloaf rest at room temperature for 10–15 minutes before cutting.

Spicy Pork

Place the pork in a slow cooker. In a bowl, mix all the seasonings and the liquids. Pour the mixture over and around the pork, then turn the setting on low.

Cook for 8 hours, or until the meat is fully cooked and tender.

With two forks, shred the pork; mix with some of the liquid and serve.

Serve with refried beans and rice. For extra flavor, cook the rice with some of the same liquid.

Serves 6.

3 pounds pork shoulder roast
1 onion, peeled and chopped
2 cloves garlic, peeled and smashed
1 bay leaf
1 small sprig rosemary
pinch of dried thyme
salt and pepper to taste
½ cup cilantro
1 16-ounce jar green salsa
2–3 serrano chili peppers
1 tablespoon butter
¼ cup ham stock, or 1 tablespoon dry ham base
¼ cup water

Tandoori Chicken

4 skinned chicken breasts
3 tablespoons tandoori mix
4 tablespoons plain yogurt
3 tablespoons white vinegar
3 tablespoons lemon juice
3 tablespoons extra virgin olive oil (plus 2 if using a skillet)

Thoroughly blend tandoori mix, yogurt, vinegar, lemon juice, and olive oil.

Rub chicken with the mixture, cover with plastic wrap, and refrigerate for 2–3 hours.

Cook on a hot grill 10–15 minutes each side.

If using a skillet, preheat oil and cook chicken until fully cooked (light brown and crispy on the outside), turning a few times.

Serve with rice and salad.

TIP: For a cold version, cut the cooked chicken into strips and serve over mixed greens, topped with your favorite dressing, and with a sprinkle of fresh grated cheese.

Seafood

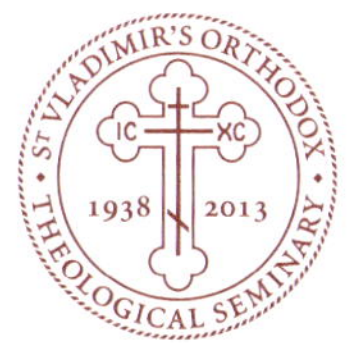

ST VLADIMIR'S ORTHODOX
THEOLOGICAL SEMINARY
IC XC
1938 2013

Almond Crusted Halibut

4 (6 ounce) pieces rinsed halibut
2 teaspoons olive oil
2 teaspoons melted butter
2 teaspoons lemon juice
4 tablespoons slivered almonds, lightly toasted and divided
salt and pepper to taste
1 teaspoon fresh dill

Preheat oven to 400F.

Place halibut in a greased baking pan.

Finely chop 2 tablespoons of almonds. Mix together chopped almonds, oil, butter, lemon juice, dill, salt, and pepper, and brush the mixture onto the fish, using the entire mixture.

Bake for 10–15 minutes or until fish flakes easily with a fork.

Sprinkle fish with the remainder of the slivered almonds, and garnish with lemon wedges and fresh dill.

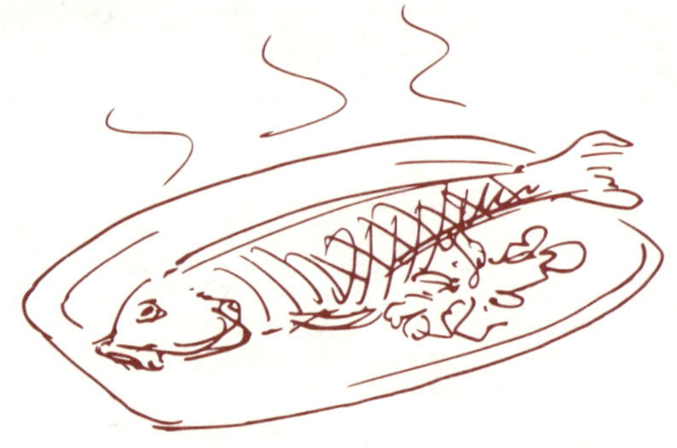

Baked Codfish

4 6-ounce portions codfish, rinsed
2 tablespoon butter, melted
1 tablespoon olive oil
1 teaspoon Old Bay seasoning
¼ teaspoon dried dill
salt and pepper to taste

Preheat oven to 375F.

Place fish in a greased baking pan.

In a small bowl, whisk together all the other ingredients,

Brush the fish with mixture, and bake for 20–25 minutes or until fish flakes.

Serves 4.

TIP: Serve with risotto.

Baked Salmon Crusted with Sesame Seeds

4 pieces salmon fillets (6 ounces each)
2 tablespoons olive oil, plus 2 more for searing
4 tablespoons sesame seeds
Kosher salt and black pepper to taste
juice of 1 lemon

Preheat oven to 375F.

In a small bowl, mix 2 tablespoons oil, salt, pepper, and lemon juice. Brush the mixture all over the fish.

In a separate shallow plate, place the sesame seeds and coat well each piece of fish.

In a skillet, heat 2 tablespoons oil (but not to smoking hot!), and sear each piece of salmon on both sides.

Bake in an oiled baking pan for 7–8 minutes or until done.

Serve with risotto and steamed cauliflower.

TIP: After salmon is cooked, drizzle with balsamic reduction sauce—it's easy to make, or it can be purchased.

Baked Lemon Dill Flounder

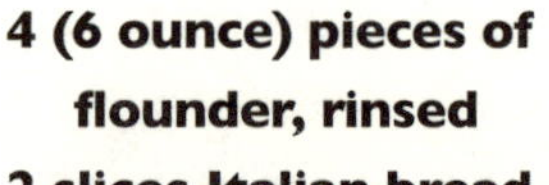

4 (6 ounce) pieces of flounder, rinsed
2 slices Italian bread, well toasted, without crusts
6 saltine crackers
¼ teaspoon paprika
2 teaspoons fresh chopped dill
1 teaspoon lemon garlic seasoning
salt and pepper to taste
juice of one lemon
2 tablespoons butter, melted

Preheat oven to 375F.

Place fish in greased baking pan, brush with melted butter.

In a food processor, process toasted bread, crackers, paprika, dill, and garlic seasoning. Top flounder with crumbs and sprinkle with lemon juice and a pinch of salt and pepper. Bake for 15 minutes or until fish flakes easily with a fork.

Serve with lemon wedges and a sprig of fresh dill.

TIP: Other fish can work well, such as codfish, scrod, grey sole, or tilapia. Just remember to adjust the time and temperature, depending on thickness of fish.

Serves 4.

Frutti Di Mare (Seafood Salad)

10 ounces of squid (calamari) rings and tentacles

1 teaspoon Kosher salt

1 bay leaf

½ teaspoon Old Bay seasoning

12 jumbo shrimp, cleaned and deveined

2 dozen medium-size mussels in shells

2 dozen clams (Little Necks) in shells

1 cup white wine

1 fennel bulb

1 teaspoon fresh parsley

FOR THE DRESSING

½ cup extra virgin olive oil

4 tablespoons fresh lemon juice

1 clove garlic, finely minced

salt and pepper to taste

1 teaspoon green sprigs from the fennel

Rinse the squid and drain. Bring a pot of water to a boil and add Kosher salt, bay leaf, and Old Bay seasoning. Add the squid and cook for 8–10 minutes, until tender; with a slotted spoon, remove the squid and place in a bowl. Repeat the same process with the shrimp until nice and pink, about 3–4 minutes. Drain and add to the bowl with the squid.

Wash and scrub the mussels and clams and place them in a pot with the wine; cover and steam until all the shells have opened, stirring once or twice. Discard any that do not open, then lift out all the mussels and clams—but don't save the liquid since it may be sandy! Pull all the meat out of the shells; combine with the squid and shrimp.

Cut the fennel in half crosswise, then cut into thin slices; mix with the fish.

Whisk together oil, lemon juice, garlic, fennel sprigs, salt, and pepper to taste; toss well with the fish. Place on a serving platter, and garnish with chopped parsley and wedges of lemon.

Grilled Shrimp & Veggie Kabobs

- **16 large shrimp (preferably U 16), cleaned and deveined**
- **16 cherry tomatoes**
- **2 medium red onions, quartered**
- **1 red bell pepper cut in 1-inch squares**
- **1 green zucchini, cut in ½-inch rounds**
- **½ cup of any Italian dressing (for the marinade)**
- **8–9-inch wooden or bamboo skewers (soaked in water for 20 minutes)**

Wash shrimp and vegetables and place in container with marinade; refrigerate for 20 minutes.

Preheat grill for 10 minutes on medium high.

Thread shrimp and vegetables alternately onto skewers.

Grill kabobs for 5–8 minutes, brushing several times with some of the marinade, turning once or twice. When fully cooked, served over mixed baby greens.

Makes 8 kabobs.

Herring

- **2 herring**
- **2 cucumbers, sliced in rounds**
- **¾ pound butter**
- **2 tablespoons fresh chopped parsley**

Soak the herring in milk for one hour, then cut each fillet into 2 strips. Decorate with rounds of cucumbers, and sprinkle with fresh parsley. Serve with butter on the side.

Lobster Chowder

2 cups lobster meat
1 medium size onion, peeled and minced
1 clove garlic, peeled minced
2 medium size white potatoes, peeled and chopped into small pieces
1 stalk celery, chopped into small pieces
1 medium carrot, peeled and chopped into small pieces
2 tablespoons olive oil
1 tablespoon butter
1 cup dry white wine
2 cups milk
1 can evaporated milk
Kosher salt and pepper to taste
2 tablespoons chopped parsley
pinch of paprika

Heat oil and butter in a sauce pot. Sauté onions and garlic, then add potatoes, celery, and carrots. Stir and cook for 2–3 minutes, then add all the liquids and keep cooking and stirring.

When the vegetables are tender, add lobster meat, season with salt and pepper, reduce heat to low, and simmer for 8–10 minutes. Add parsley, sprinkle with paprika, stir, and serve hot.

Serves 4.

Polish Style Mussels

4–5 dozen fresh mussels, scrubbed and rinsed
1½ pounds of kielbasa sausage, cut in ½-inch rounds
3 tablespoons extra virgin olive oil
3 cloves garlic, peeled and chopped
½ cup dry red wine
4 medium size peeled tomatoes, seeded and chopped
6 fresh basil leaves, cut in half
1 tablespoon chopped fresh parsley
salt and black pepper to taste
crushed hot red pepper to taste

In a hot skillet, heat the oil, then add kielbasa and sauté for a few minutes. Add the garlic, then cook for few seconds; add the wine and keep cooking until the wine evaporates. Add tomatoes and continue to cook over low medium heat, 10–12 minutes. Add mussels and remaining seasonings and herbs. Cover and cook 12–15 minutes until all mussels have opened. Discard the ones that didn't open, and serve.

Serves 6.

Paella

In a large pot over medium-high heat, heat oil. Add onion and cook for 2–3 minutes until soft, then add the garlic and the butter. Add pork and chicken, and cook until the meat starts to brown.

Add the oregano, paprika, garlic-pepper, chopped tomatoes, chicken stock, and yellow rice. Bring to a boil and simmer.

In a separate pot, steam mussels and clams in white wine until they open (discard the ones that don't open), remove the mussels and clams from their shells and set aside.

Add shrimp to the rice, then the green peas, and cook until shrimp turns pink. Keep simmering until the rice is soft and the meat is fully cooked. Add mussels and clams to the mixture, toss together, and add more liquid as needed.

TIP: Add crushed hot red pepper if desired!

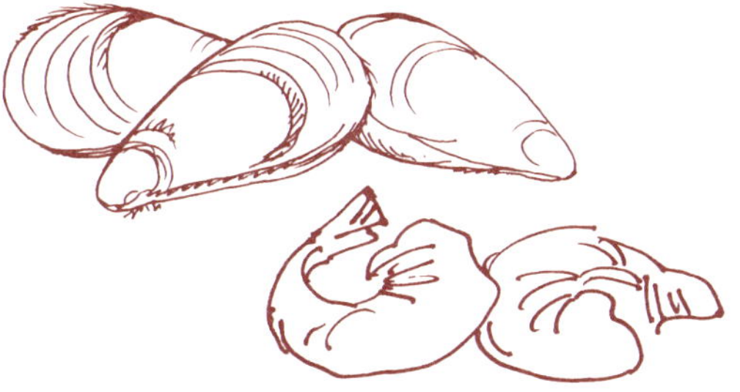

3 tablespoons olive oil
1½ onions, chopped
3 cloves garlic, crushed and chopped
1 28-ounce can chopped tomatoes
1½ cups yellow rice (Spanish style)
1 teaspoon oregano
½ teaspoon paprika
½ teaspoon garlic-pepper (optional)
1 pound boneless chicken, cut in 1-2-inch pieces
1 pound boneless lean pork, cut in 1 inch-pieces
12 mussels, cleaned
12 small clams
1 pound medium shrimp, cleaned and deveined
1 cup fresh or frozen peas
1 teaspoon butter
1 cup white wine
2 cups chicken stock
salt and pepper to taste

Red Snapper Al Cartoccio

2 red snapper fillets
1 small carrot, chopped
1 green onion, chopped
½ stalk celery, chopped
1 teaspoon garlic pepper
2 cloves garlic, smashed
3 tablespoons white wine
2 sprigs fresh parsley
1 sprig fresh tarragon
salt and pepper to taste

Heat grill to about 400F.

Rinse the fish and place the fillets on a large piece of aluminum foil. Add all the seasonings, wine, and vegetables and close the aluminum foil, forming it like a closed basket.

Cook on the grill top for 15–20 minutes, or until the fish is tender and fully cooked.

Unwrap the foil; the skin should easily peel off. Serve, with vegetables as garnish.

Salmon Al Cartoccio (packet)

- **1 3-pound piece salmon fillet**
- **1 leek—the white part only, chopped**
- **1 bay leaf**
- **½ large carrot, cut in chunks**
- **1 celery stick, cut in chunks**
- **3 tablespoons white wine**
- **salt and pepper to taste**
- **1 teaspoon Old Bay seasoning**
- **1 tablespoon butter**
- **2 lemons, sliced**
- **2–3 sprigs fresh parsley**

Preheat oven to 375F.

Lightly grease one piece of aluminum foil, large enough to wrap the fish.

Place the salmon on the foil; add seasoning, vegetables, and wine.

Form a packet around the fish with the foil and seal it.

Place the packet in a baking pan, and bake for 25–30 minutes, until the salmon is cooked as you like it.

Open foil and serve hot. Use same process if using the grill.

TIP: Other types of fish may be used with the same recipe.

Salmon Made Easy

1 3-pound piece salmon fillet
½ teaspoon Old Bay seasoning
pinch black pepper
½ teaspoon chopped fresh dill
2 tablespoons butter
2 sliced lemons
2 lemons, cut into wedges

Preheat oven to 350F.

Lightly grease a baking dish large enough for the salmon to fit. Place the sliced lemons on the base of the dish; place the salmon on top of lemons.

Mix Old Bay seasoning, black pepper, and dill, and spread evenly over the fish; dot with butter.

Bake for 25–30 minutes, or until the salmon looks and feels done. Serve in the same dish, and garnish with sprigs of fresh dill and lemon wedges.

Serve with plain steamed rice and your favorite salad.

Serves 6.

Seafood Cioppino (mild version)

In a large pot over medium heat, sauté onion, garlic, and both bell peppers in oil until tender. Add salt and pepper, basil, oregano, thyme, crushed tomatoes, tomato sauce, water, paprika, and clam juice.

Stir well, reduce heat, and simmer 1–2 hours. Add the wine a little at a time.

20 minutes before serving, add clams, mussels, shrimps, scallops, and cod.

Cover for the last 10 minutes, but keep stirring as needed.

When the seafood in fully cooked, the mussels should be open (if not then discard), the shrimp should be pink, and the cod should be flaky.

TIP: Goes well with rice pilaf or risotto.

¼ cup olive oil
1 onion, chopped
3 cloves garlic, minced
1 green bell pepper
1 red bell pepper
½ cup chopped parsley
1 teaspoon dried basil
1 teaspoon dried oregano
pinch dried thyme
1 28-ounce can crushed tomatoes
1 cup tomato sauce
½ cup water
pinch paprika
1 cup dry white wine
1 cup minced clams, rinsed
1 cup clam juice
24 jumbo shrimp
24 medium-sized mussels, cleaned
1 pound scallops
1 pound cod fillets, cut into 1-inch-pieces
Salt and pepper to taste

Seafood Lo Mein

1 tablespoon cornstarch
¾ teaspoon fresh grated ginger
¼ cup soy sauce
1 teaspoon fish base (or chicken base)
1 pound shrimp (medium), cleaned and deveined
¾ pound sea scallops, rinsed
½ cup white wine
½ pound linguine
½ pound mushrooms, sliced
¼ pound fresh snow peas
1 red bell pepper, seeded and julienned
2 green onions, chopped
2 tablespoons vegetable oil, divided
2 teaspoons sesame oil
1 tablespoon chopped parsley
black pepper to taste

In a bowl, combine cornstarch, ginger, soy sauce; add shrimp and scallops and toss well to combine.

In a large skillet, heat a tablespoon of vegetable oil, then stir-fry the mushrooms, peppers, and snow peas until crisp (2-3 minutes). With slotted spoon remove the vegetables and set aside. With remainder of the oil, stir-fry the fish, then add wine, fish base, green onions, and sesame oil.

Add the rest of the vegetables and toss. Keep stirring and cooking until the fish is fully cooked, about 5–6 minutes (if sauce is too thick, add water).

Add parsley, a pinch of black pepper, then toss and serve.

TIP: Serve with steamed sushi rice.

Serves 6.

Shrimp Creole

Separately, prepare sufficient rice for the number of persons who will be sharing this meal.

In a hot skillet, heat oil, then sauté onions and garlic for one minute. Add green pepper and celery and cook for 2–3 minutes; then add plum tomatoes, tomato sauce, bay leaf, Tabasco, Creole seasoning, salt, and pepper. Bring to a boil.

Toss flour with shrimp, then add shrimp to the boiling sauce and cook for 5–6 minutes or until shrimp is fully cooked. Remove bay leaf, and serve with rice.

2 pounds jumbo shrimp, peeled and deveined

1 tablespoon vegetable oil

1 onion, peeled and minced

1 clove garlic, peeled and minced

1 green bell pepper, seeded and chopped

2 stalks celery, rinsed and chopped

2 tablespoons flour

1 tablespoon Creole seasoning

1 bay leaf

4 plum tomatoes, rinsed and chopped

1 cup tomato sauce

1 teaspoon Tabasco sauce

Kosher salt and pepper to taste

Shrimp, Scallops & Banana Soup

8 green bananas
1 pound large shrimp, peeled and deveined
¾ pound scallops, rinsed
½ teaspoon salt
1 lemon, cut in half
1 large tomato, peeled, seeded, and diced
1 onion, chopped
2 Scotch bonnet peppers, finely chopped
1 sprig fresh thyme
4 teaspoons Pickapeppa sauce
1 teaspoon Old Bay seasoning

Peel bananas and cut them into quarters, set aside.

Bring 1¾ quarts of water to a boil. Add lemon, salt, Old Bay seasoning, the shrimp, and scallops, and cook for about 3–4 minutes. Add tomato, onion, Scotch bonnet, thyme, and Pickapeppa sauce, and half the cut bananas, and cook over medium heat for 15–20 minutes.

Remove the lemon and discard.

When soup is ready, scoop into serving bowls and top with the remainder of the bananas, and serve.

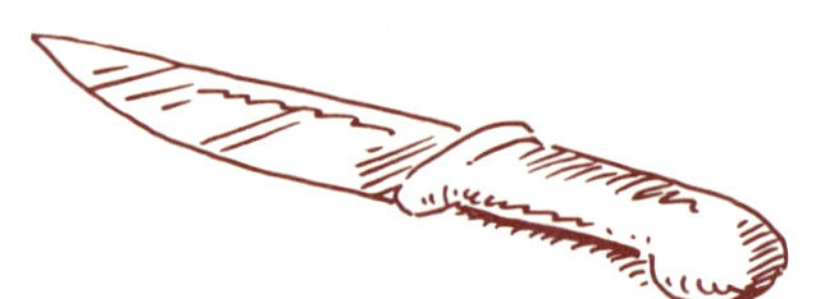

Snow Crab Clusters on the Grill

¾ cup extra virgin olive oil
½ cup butter plus ¾ cup melted butter for dipping
¼ cup fresh minced garlic
pinch paprika
4–5 pounds snow crab clusters

Whisk together the olive oil, butter, garlic, and paprika, then generously brush onto crab.

Cook the crab on a preheated grill on high, turning once or twice, until the shell begins to brown, about 6–8 minutes.

Serve with melted butter and wedges of lemon.

Serves 4–6.

Desserts

ST VLADIMIR'S ORTHODOX
THEOLOGICAL SEMINARY
IC XC
1938 2013

Apple Crisp

2 cups all-purpose flour
2 cups rolled oats
1 ⅓ teaspoons cinnamon
¾ teaspoon ground nutmeg
1 ½ cups brown sugar
1 ¼ cups butter, room temperature
2 quarts peeled, cored, and sliced Granny Smith apples

Preheat oven to 350F.

Combine the flour, oats, cinnamon, nutmeg, and brown sugar in a mixing bowl. Cut butter in small pieces and add to mixture until crumbly.

Evenly spread half the mixture in the bottom of a lightly greased 9×13 baking pan, lightly pressing down; top evenly with sliced apples and cover the apples with the rest of the mixture.

Bake for about 50 minutes or until apples are tender.

Serve with ice cream.

Apple Enchiladas

3 cups apple pie filling
6 flour tortillas
1 teaspoon ground cinnamon
⅓ cup margarine
½ cup granulated sugar
½ cup brown sugar
½ cup water
powdered sugar and fresh mint leaves for garnish

Preheat oven to 350F.

Divide apple pie filling among the tortillas and sprinkle each with a pinch of cinnamon. Roll each tortilla and place seam-side down in a greased 8×8 baking pan.

Bring water, margarine, and sugar to a boil, reduce heat, simmer, and stir constantly for about 3 minutes. Pour sauce over tortillas, then sprinkle with pinch of cinnamon and bake for 20–25 minutes.

Place on a serving platter; sprinkle with powdered sugar and garnish with fresh mint leaves; serve warm.

For better presentation, cut diagonally in halves or thirds.

Apple Strudel

1 puff pastry sheet (12×16)
2 tablespoons granulated sugar
1 tablespoon all-purpose flour
½ teaspoon ground cinnamon
2 large Granny Smith apples, peeled, cored, and thinly sliced
2 tablespoons golden raisins
1 egg and 1 tablespoon water (for the egg wash)

Preheat oven to 375F.

Mix together the sugar, flour, cinnamon, and the raisins, toss with the apples to coat evenly.

Spread the pastry sheet on a baking pan and pour the apple mixture over the sheet 1 inch from the edge. Roll it like a jelly roll and keep the seam side down; tuck the ends under to seal.

Brush with egg-wash and bake for about 35–40 minutes or until golden brown, then cool before serving,

For garnish, sprinkle with powdered sugar and a mint leaf.

Works well with ice cream.

Bacon Oatmeal Cookies

1 cup margarine or butter, softened
2 cups packed brown sugar
1 cup white sugar
2 eggs
2 teaspoons vanilla extract
1½ cups all-purpose flour
2 teaspoons baking soda
1 teaspoon nutmeg
1 teaspoon ground cinnamon
7 cups quick oats
2 cups raisins
2 cups chopped walnuts
1 cup chocolate chips
1 pound bacon, well done: crispy and fine, and chopped in food processor
½ teaspoon salt

Preheat oven to 350F.

In a mixing bowl, cream the margarine or the butter with the brown and white sugar, 3–4 minutes until blended.

Stir in eggs, vanilla extract, flour, baking soda, nutmeg, ground cinnamon, raisins, and chopped walnuts, and then chocolate chips, bacon, and salt.

Slowly pour in the quick oats until well-mixed, and keep mixing for an additional 4–5 minutes.

Drop dough in full teaspoons, 2 inches apart, onto a greased sheet pan.

Bake 12–14 minutes or until medium light brown—not too dark!

After baking, let cool for 15 minutes in cookie pan before removing.

TIP: Add oats for a harder mixture.

Baked Bananas 151

4 large bananas, peeled and sliced lengthwise
fresh-squeezed juice of 2 limes
2 tablespoons 151 rum
2 tablespoons brown sugar
dash cinnamon and nutmeg
1 tablespoon melted butter
4 large scoops of vanilla ice cream

Preheat oven to 400F.

With some of the butter, grease a baking pan and set aside.

Mix together the rum, brown sugar, cinnamon, nutmeg, and lime juice. Place bananas face down in the pan, brush them with remainder of butter, pour the rum mixture over the bananas, and bake for 10–15 minutes until some of the liquid is absorbed.

With a spatula, place two pieces of banana in a serving dish with ice cream and serve hot.

Garnish with fresh mint leaves.

Serves 4.

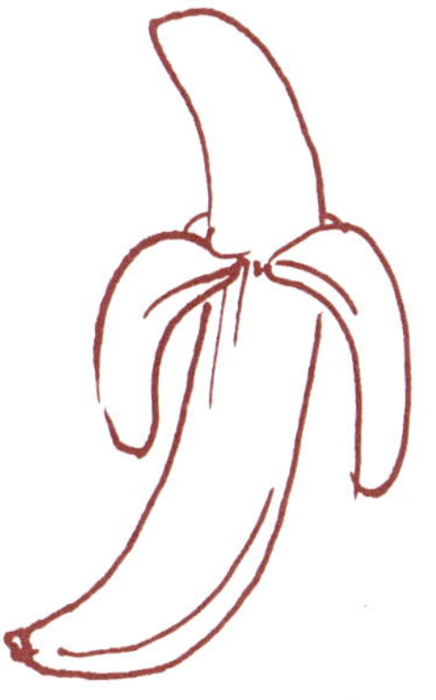

Basic Pound Cake (Pane Di Spagna)

3 cups flour
1 teaspoon baking powder
½ teaspoon baking soda
½ teaspoon salt
1 cup butter, softened
2 cups sugar
2 teaspoons vanilla extract
5 large eggs
1 cup milk
1 teaspoon almond extract

Grease and flour a10-inch tube pan, set aside.

Preheat oven to 350F.

Sift the flour, baking powder, baking soda, and salt in a large bowl. In a separate bowl, beat the butter, sugar, vanilla, and almond extract until creamy; now start adding the eggs one at a time, beating until all blend in.

Reduce speed to low and gradually beat in the dry ingredients, alternating with the milk, until smooth.

Pour the mixture into the prepared pan and bake for about 1 hour, or until a toothpick comes out clean and dry.

Once done, let it rest for 10–15 minutes to cool; run a knife around the inner edge to loosen, and remove from pan. Top with your favorite icing (optional) and serve.

Basic Zabaglione

4 egg yolks
¼ cup sugar
½ cup marsala wine (dry or sweet, depending on preference)

In the top portion of a double boiler, on high speed, beat eggs and sugar until smooth and thick.

Gradually add the marsala. Continue to cook over very low simmering water, 10–15 minutes, stirring constantly.

TIP: Try using ¼ cup of the marsala and ¼ cup espresso coffee.

Can be served alone or as a filling, or as topping over fresh fruit or ice cream.

Blueberry Cobbler

½ stick butter
3 cups sugar
4 cups self-rising flour
4 cups milk
4 cups fresh or frozen blueberries

Preheat oven to 350F.

Melt butter, and use it to grease an 18×13 baking pan; leave the extra butter in pan.

In a sauce pot, cook blueberries until soft and mushy, about 13–15 minutes.

Mix together sugar, flour, and milk, using a whisk.

Pour the mixture into the pan and spread the cooked blueberries evenly on top.

Bake 50–60 minutes or until a toothpick comes out clean.

Serve warm or at room temperature.

TIP: Works well with ice cream or whipped cream.

Caramel-dipped Oranges

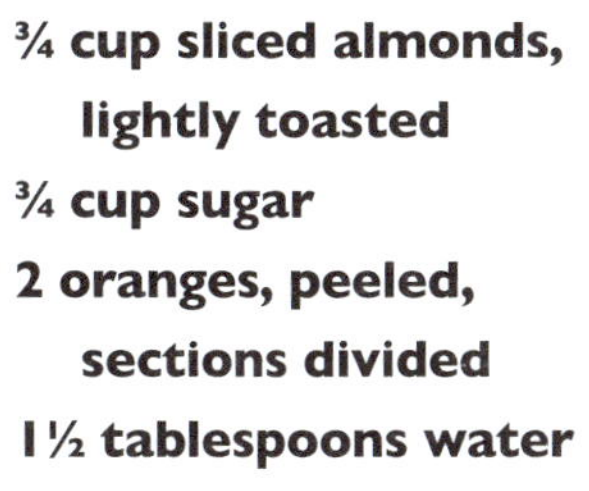

¾ cup sliced almonds, lightly toasted

¾ cup sugar

2 oranges, peeled, sections divided

1½ tablespoons water

In a small sauce pan, gently mix sugar and water, cooking over low heat without stirring, until caramel is a light golden brown, about 9–10 minutes.

Remove from heat and carefully dip one side of each orange slice into the caramel, and then place it on serving platter, caramel side up.

Sprinkle with toasted almonds.

Garnish with a fresh mint leaf.

Serve with a scoop of vanilla ice cream.

Caribbean Sweet Potato Pone

2 pounds sweet potatoes, peeled and grated
1½ cups milk
2 cups cream of coconut
1¾ cups light brown sugar
2 teaspoons vanilla extract
1½ teaspoons ground ginger
1½ teaspoons ground cinnamon
¾ teaspoon fresh grated nutmeg
½ cup raisins
½ cup coconut flakes
2½ cups hot water
2 tablespoons melted butter

Preheat oven to 375F.

In a buttered casserole dish, combine sweet potatoes and milk.

In a bowl, combine cream of coconut, sugar, vanilla, and the rest of the spices, and mix well.

Add raisins, coconut flakes, hot water, and butter.

Mix thoroughly, adding more sugar, if needed. Pour into the casserole with the sweet-potatoes-and-milk mixture, and bake for about 50–60 minutes until set.

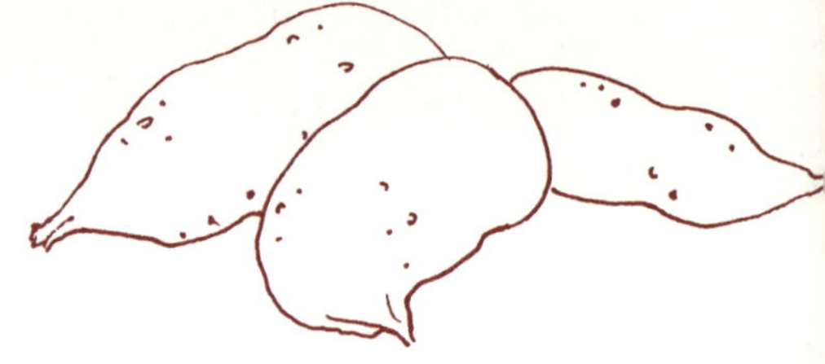

Do not burn! Check after 40 minutes.

Gianduja (Chocolate Hazelnut)

5 ounces hazelnuts
8 ounces milk chocolate
¼ cup demerara sugar
½ teaspoon Kosher salt
¼ cup grapeseed oil

In a 350F oven or on stove top, toast hazelnuts until they are light brown and the skins are loose. If using stove top, make sure to toss frequently. Wrap nuts in cloth napkin and rub together so that some of the skin comes off. If some of the skin remains, it's ok.

While the nuts are still warm, combine them with milk chocolate, sugar, and salt in a food processor. Purée until smooth, slowly adding oil in a steady stream.

Transfer the mixture to an airtight container; let it stand at room temperature until thickened, about 2 days. Gianduja holds well at room temperature for a few weeks. If too chilled, heat in microwave for 5 seconds.

Grilled Banana Boat

4 bananas (cut a piece away from outer curve, so they don't roll over)
4 pieces aluminum foil (to wrap the bananas)
2 tablespoons soft butter
3 tablespoons chocolate chips
1 tablespoon sugar
whipped cream
rainbow sprinkles
chopped nuts
pitted cherries
vanilla and chocolate ice cream
crumbled Oreo cookies
1 ounce Crème de menthe, or Amaretto di Saronno, or Sambuca (optional)

Preheat grill and place each banana on aluminum foil with cut ends facing down. Cut a slit lengthwise over the top, gently open, and brush with butter. Sprinkle the chocolate chips (inside banana skins), wrap with aluminum foil, and cook over a hot grill for about 7–8 minutes. Let cool for a few minutes and then unwrap the foil. Top each banana with all the toppings.

TIP: Adults may enjoy drizzling liqueurs over this dessert!

Jamaican Crunchy Snack

1 cup all-purpose flour
¼ teaspoon baking soda
1 cup sugar
½ teaspoon nutmeg
¼ teaspoon salt
1 cup shredded coconut (unsweetened)
3–4 tablespoons water

Preheat oven to 375F.

Combine the flour, soda, sugar, nutmeg, and salt; add coconut, and mix. Add water and mix well to form a thick dough. On a floured counter, roll out the dough to ⅛ -inch thick.

Cut the dough in the shape of rectangles and place them on a greased baking sheet. Bake for 9–10 minutes. Let cool and serve.

Makes 18–20 pieces.

Mango Caribbean

4 large, ripe mangos, peeled
2 cups whipping cream
2 cups plain yogurt
brown sugar

Cut mangos into slices and lay them in a serving bowl, or divide them into individual mugs. Beat cream until thick and then fold in yogurt; beat again until lump-free. Pour over mango slices and sprinkle liberally with brown sugar.

Refrigerate 4–5 hours before serving.

Garnish with fresh mint leaves.

Mango Sherbet

1 cup sugar
1¼ ounces unflavored gelatin
1½ cups boiling water
1½ cups mango purée (2–3 mangos)
1 cup milk
2 tablespoons fresh lime juice
2 egg whites

In a large bowl, mix ¾ cup of sugar and gelatin. Add boiling water, stirring until the sugar and gelatin are completely dissolved. Cool to room temperature.

Stir in the mango purée, milk, and lime juice, then place bowl in freezer for 1½ hours or until the mixture is frozen about ½ inches around side of bowl. Beat with a whisk until smooth.

In a separate bowl, beat egg whites with remaining ¼ cup sugar until stiff peaks form, then fold into mango mixture; return to freezer several hours or until firm.

NOTE: Contains raw egg whites.

Multi-berry Crisp

1½ cups fresh blueberries
1½ cups blackberries
1½ cups raspberries
2 tablespoons balsamic vinegar
2 tablespoons white vinegar
2 cups flour
2 cups rolled oats
1½ cups brown sugar
½ teaspoon ground cinnamon
½ teaspoon ground nutmeg
1½ cups butter
¼ teaspoon salt
¼ teaspoon baking soda

Preheat oven to 350F.

In a large bowl, toss together all the berries and both vinegars. In a separate bowl mix together the oats, flour, sugar, cinnamon, nutmeg, salt, and baking soda. Pinch in the butter until crumbly mixture is created.

Spread and press half of the mixture in the bottom of a 9×13 pan, cover evenly with berries, and spread the rest of the crumble over the top.

Bake for 40–45 minutes or until it bubbles and the top is golden brown.

Let rest for 10–15 minutes before slicing; garnish with fresh mint leaves and a few fresh berries.

TIP: It goes well with vanilla ice cream or fresh whipped cream.

New Zealand Lamingtons or Sponge Cake Squares

½ cup butter
¾ cup sugar
1 teaspoon vanilla extract
2 large eggs
2 cups flour
2 tablespoons baking powder
¼ teaspoon salt
½ cup milk
4 cups powdered sugar
⅓ cup cocoa powder
2 tablespoons melted butter
½ cup milk
16 ounces dried coconut flakes

Preheat oven to 375F.

Grease and flour an 8×12 pan. Sift together flour, baking powder, and salt.

Cream ½ cup butter, ¾ cup sugar, and vanilla until fluffy.

Add the eggs one at a time; add the flour mixture and milk slowly, and beat well.

Pour the batter into the pan, bake for about 35–45 minutes, until a toothpick comes out clean.

Let it cool completely, overnight if possible.

Make the icing by combining powdered sugar and cocoa powder in a small pot; in a separate pot heat milk and butter until butter is melted. Add milk to the cocoa mixture and mix well to form runny icing (not too thick). Cut cake into 1½-inch squares. Then, with a fork or a skewer, dip the pieces of cake into the icing, then into coconut flakes, and place them on a rack so the excess can run off.

Serve as a sweet snack.

Panna Cotta

1 cup fat-free milk
2 tablespoons unflavored gelatin
8 cups heavy cream
1½ cups sugar
2 tablespoons vanilla extract
1 teaspoon almond extract
cocoa powder for garnish

Mix sugar and cream together and bring to boil, stirring occasionally.

Mix gelatin with fat-free milk, stir, and mix into the cream. Cook for 1 minute, take off the stove, and add vanilla and almond extract; mix well.

Divide into 20 ramekins or stemmed wine glasses, and cool at room temperature; cover each with plastic wrap and chill in refrigerator (best overnight).

Sprinkle some cocoa powder on top and serve.

Makes 20 portions.

Peach Cobbler

4 cups peeled, sliced peaches
2 cups sugar, divided
½ cup water
4 tablespoons butter, melted
1½ cups self-rising flour
1½ cups milk
pinch ground cinnamon and ground nutmeg
2 tablespoons vanilla extract
mint leaves for garnish

Preheat oven to 350F.

Mix together peaches, half the sugar, the water, and the vanilla; bring to a boil for about 10 minutes, then let cool for a few minutes.

Spread butter on the base of a 3-quart baking pan.

Mix the remaining sugar, flour, and milk, whisk well to prevent lumps.

Pour the batter into the greased baking pan, spoon in the peaches, and spoon all the juices evenly over the top (do not stir). Sprinkle with nutmeg and cinnamon.

Bake for about 35–40 minutes, or until golden brown and firm.

Cool to room temperature, and serve with vanilla ice cream and whipped cream, and garnish with fresh mint leaves.

Puerto Rican Rum Ball

2½ cups vanilla wafer crumbs
1 cup chopped walnuts
½ cup rum
1 tablespoon corn syrup
1 cup powdered sugar
walnuts, finely chopped (optional)
cocoa powder (optional)

Mix vanilla wafer crumbs and walnuts. Place the remaining ingredients in a separate bowl and blend well with mixer. Combine all the ingredients. Make one-inch-diameter balls from the batter, and roll each ball in the powdered sugar, finely chopped walnuts, or cocoa powder.

South American Cookies

⅓ cup shortening
½ cup brown sugar
½ cup granulated sugar
1 egg
1½ teaspoons vanilla extract
1 tablespoon milk
2 cups flour
½ teaspoon salt
¼ teaspoon baking powder
¼ teaspoon baking soda
2 tablespoons instant coffee

Preheat oven to 400F.

Mix shortening, sugar, egg, vanilla, and milk until fluffy. Mix the dry ingredients in a separate bowl, then add to the liquid mixture. Combine thoroughly until blended, then shape into 1-inch balls. Place balls 2 inches apart on a cookie tray. Flatten to ⅛ inch thick by pressing down with the bottom of a glass dipped in sugar. Bake about 8–10 minutes.

Sweet Feast

1 cup pecans, chopped
1 cup flour
½ cup butter
4 tablespoons sugar
8 ounces cream cheese
½ cup powdered sugar (also called confectioners' sugar)
2 cups Cool Whip, divided
2 cups milk
1 package vanilla instant pudding
1 package chocolate instant pudding
½ cup shaved chocolate chips (for topping)

Preheat oven to 350F.

Mix together pecans, flour, butter, sugar; press down into a baking pan about 10×12 in size.

Bake for 25–30 minutes, set aside, and let cool.

Mix together cream cheese, powdered sugar, one cup Cool Whip; spread over the crust.

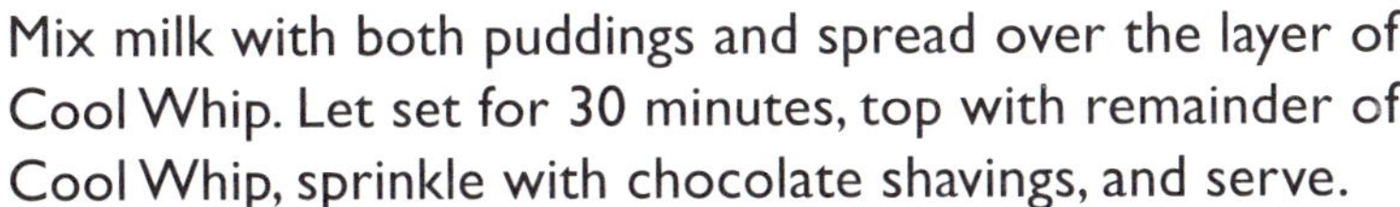

Mix milk with both puddings and spread over the layer of Cool Whip. Let set for 30 minutes, top with remainder of Cool Whip, sprinkle with chocolate shavings, and serve.

Garnish with fresh mint leaves.

Tropical Fruit Shake

1 ripe and sweet pineapple, peeled, cored, and cut in chunks
2 mangos, peeled, pitted, cut in chunks
4 bananas, peeled and sliced
1 pound strawberries, washed
vanilla ice cream
orange juice
grenadine for color (optional)

Mix together ingredients; pour into a blender, process in multiple batches.

Adjust the amount of liquids according to your preference.

Serve chilled.

Turkish Coffee Cake

1 cup brown sugar
2 cups whole wheat flour
½ cup butter
2–3 tablespoons instant coffee
2 teaspoons cinnamon
½ teaspoon nutmeg
1 teaspoon baking soda
1 teaspoon allspice
1 cup sour cream
1 egg, beaten
½ cup chopped nuts

Preheat oven to 350F.

Mix dry ingredients except baking soda and nuts. Cut in butter with pastry cutter until crumbly. Press half of the mixture into a 9×13 pan. Mix the remaining half with sour cream, egg, soda, and chopped nuts, and pour on top.

Bake 25–30 minutes.

Serve with Turkish (Greek, Serbian, etc.) coffee on the side.

Virgin Island Parfaits

In food processor, blend banana and orange juice.

In a bowl, combine pineapple, papaya, mangos, and half banana mixture; toss it well.

Divide mixed fruit into six serving glasses, top each with the rest of banana sauce, grated coconut, and two cherries.

TIP: Garnish with fresh mint leaves and an orange slice on each glass rim.

1 medium ripe pineapple, peeled, cored, and cubed (small)
2 papayas, peeled, seeded, and cubed
2 mangos, peeled, pitted, and cubed
1–2 bananas
½ cup fresh-squeezed orange juice
¾ cup fresh-grated coconut
12 pitted cherries

Zeppole

Preheat oil to 375F.

Beat the eggs slightly; add flour, baking powder, sugar, ricotta cheese, vanilla, salt, and chocolate drops (optional). Combine all the ingredients together; the batter will look and feel sticky. Drop a teaspoon of batter into hot oil, turning once until golden brown, about 3–4 minutes (make in small batches,).

Drain on a paper towel and roll in powdered sugar; serve warm or at room temperature.

2 cups all-purpose flour
4 eggs
4 teaspoons baking powder
3 teaspoons sugar
2 cups ricotta cheese
1 teaspoon vanilla extract
vegetable oil for frying
pinch of salt
¼ cup chocolate drops (optional)

Recipes by Type

Breads

Appetizers

Breakfast

Soup

Pasta & Rice

Vegetables

Meat

Seafood

Desserts

Recipes by Title